CfE
Curriculum for Excellence

Exploring People and Society

Gemma Ritchie

Series Editor: Ollie Bray

DYNAMIC LEARNING

HODDER GIBSON

The Publishers would like to thank the following for permission to reproduce copyright material:

Photo credits
p.2 Demotix/Press Association Images; p.6 (main) © AKP Photos/Alamy, (t inset) © Olivier Asselin/Alamy, (b inset) Twitter; p.8 LE FLOCH/SIPA/Rex Features; p.9 Sipa Press/Rex Features; p.10–11 Paul Turner – Fotolia; p.14 © Vehbi Koca/Alamy; p.16 (l) © C Squared Studios/Photodisc/Getty Images; p.19 (l) © 67photo/Alamy, (r) © Sean Gladwell – Fotolia.com; p.20 © Mark Harvey/ Alamy; p.22 (t) © Jeffrey Blackler/Alamy, (b) Brian Jackson – Fotolia; p.27 (t) Sipa Press/Rex Features, (b) Hans Deryk/AP Photo/PA Images; p.29 Gudmund – Fotolia; p.31 (t) © Lifescenes/Alamy, (b) picsfive – Fotolia; p.32 (t) Conservative Party, (c) Labour Party, (b) Liberal Democrats; p.33 © Neil McAllister/Alamy; p.35 PA Wire/Press Association Images; p.37 (t) © STEVE LINDRIDGE/Alamy, (b) Tupungato – Fotolia; p.40 © Global Warming Images/Alamy; p.41 ©PA Photos/TopFoto; p.42 INS News Agency Ltd./Rex Features; p.45 (l) Siede Preis©Siede Preis/Photodisc/Getty Images, (r) © Dmitriy Chistoprudov – Fotolia.com; p.46 (l) Canadian Press/Rex Features, (r) Mercury Press Agency/Rex Features; p.49 Alastair Grant/AP Photo/PA Images; p.53 (t) © Adrian Sherratt/ Alamy, (b) © Yuri Arcurs – Fotolia.com; p.54 ©Photodisc/Getty Images; p.57 (l) ©Photodisc/Getty Images, (c) Official White House Photo by Chuck Kennedy, (r) ©Photodisc/Getty Images; p.58 Official White House Photo by Chuck Kennedy; p.59 WITT/ ALFRED/ SIPA/Rex Features; p.60 Kablonk Micro – Fotolia; p.61 (l) Startraks Photo/Rex Features, (r) Getty Images/National Geographic Creative; p.63 © Michael Ainsworth/Dallas Morning News/Corbis; p.64 Peter Kramer/AP Photo/PA Images; p.65 © amana images inc./Alamy; p.66 PA Archive/Press Association Images; p.67 (t) Getty Images/Dorling Kindersley, (b) Elinor Jones/Rex Features; p.68 © Imagestate Media (John Foxx); p.69 © erolus – Fotolia.com; p.72 © Paul Thompson Images/Alamy; p.73 PAUL ELLIS/AFP/Getty Images; p.74 (t) NATO, (b) Fulad Hamdard/AP Photo/PA Images; p.77 Hussein Malla/AP Photo/PA Images; p.78 ©FAO/Alessia Pierdomenico; p.81 AP/Press Association Images; p.82 stoonn – Fotolia; p.84 Demotix/Press Association Images; p.85 (t) Louisa Macdonell/Rex Features, (b) Susan Walsh/AP Photo/PA Images; p.86 Sunday Alamba/AP Photo/PA Images; p.87 Rex Features; p.88 Merlin; p.89 Merlin; p.90 Fairtrade Foundation; p.92 Chao Soi Cheong/AP Photo/PA Images; p.93 Sipa Press/Rex Features; p.95 (t) AP/Press Association Images, (b) © 2020WEB/Alamy; p.97 (l) Family Lives, (r) © Monkey Business – Fotolia.com; p.98 © Piotr Marcinski – Fotolia.com; p.104 (t) © Roger Cracknell 14/Asia/Alamy, (b) © digitalknight/Alamy; p.105 © CR Photography/Alamy; p.106 (main) © Stockbyte/ Getty Images Ltd, (t inset) © Elizabeth Hayes, (b inset) © Elizabeth Hayes; p.108 (l) © SoFood/Alamy; p.109 Vladimir Mucibabic – Fotolia; p.111 (tl) Demotix/Press Association Images, (tr) AP/Press Association Images, (bl) © OlgaLIS – Fotolia.com, (br) AP Photo/Koji Sasahara/PA Photos; p.112 Mark Mawson/ Robert Harding /Rex Features; p.113 PA Images; p.114 Ljupco Smokovski – Fotolia; p.115 (l) © Elizabeth Hayes, (r) THE CON/Album/akg-images; p.116 © mediablitzimages (uk) Limited/ Alamy; p.117 (l) © Claus Mikosch - Fotolia.com, (r) © Stockbyte/ Photolibrary Group Ltd; p.118 (l) © T.M.O.Buildings/Alamy, (r) © Travel Pictures/Alamy; p.119 © Edd Westmacott/Alamy.

Photos on pages 4, 12, 13, 15, 16 (r), 24, 50, 70, 71, 79 and 108 © Gemma Ritchie.

Acknowledgements
The artwork detailing the environmental impact of different types of food on p.116 is Copyright Barilla Center for Food & Nutrition and has been re-drawn with permission.

Every effort has been made to trace all copyright holders, but if any have been inadvertently overlooked the Publishers will be pleased to make the necessary arrangements at the first opportunity.

Although every effort has been made to ensure that website addresses are correct at time of going to press, Hodder Gibson cannot be held responsible for the content of any website mentioned in this book. It is sometimes possible to find a relocated web page by typing in the address of the home page for a website in the URL window of your browser.

Hachette UK's policy is to use papers that are natural, renewable and recyclable products and made from wood grown in sustainable forests. The logging and manufacturing processes are expected to conform to the environmental regulations of the country of origin.

Orders: please contact Bookpoint Ltd, 130 Milton Park, Abingdon, Oxon OX14 4SB. Telephone: (44) 01235 827720. Fax: (44) 01235 400454. Lines are open 9.00–5.00, Monday to Saturday, with a 24-hour message answering service. Visit our website at www.hoddereducation.co.uk. Hodder Gibson can be contacted direct on: Tel: 0141 848 1609; Fax: 0141 889 6315; email: hoddergibson@hodder.co.uk

© Gemma Ritchie 2012
First published in 2012 by
Hodder Gibson, an imprint of Hodder Education,
An Hachette UK Company
2a Christie Street
Paisley PA1 1NB

Impression number   5 4 3 2 1
Year   2014 2013 2012

Cover photo © Lydia Austin
Illustrations by Emma Golley at Redmoor Design and Jeff Edwards
Typeset in ITC Stone Serif 11pt by DC Graphic Design Limited, Swanley Village, Kent.
Printed in Italy

A catalogue record for this title is available from the British Library

ISBN: 978 1444 145199

Contents

1 Welcome back to Modern Studies

Modern Studies is all about studying the society around us. It is about looking at people and the way that they interact with each other. You can study the world at three different levels: local, national and international. In this book, you will be encouraged to view issues at all three levels. A local issue is one which affects your town, village or local council area. A national issue is one which affects Scotland or the UK. An international issue is one which affects a country other than Scotland or the UK. An international issue may even affect several countries, or the whole world.

Modern Studies is all about understanding how society changes, how countries are governed and how different individuals or groups influence the way in which society is run. Modern Studies will encourage you to become more open-minded and tolerant towards different ideas about how our society should operate. It will help you to develop a greater understanding of the way in which countries interact with each other and the global problems which we face. It should also make you more aware of the way in which you can participate and influence how society is run, making you a more active citizen.

One way of understanding how society around us interacts and affects us is by keeping up to date with current affairs. Current affairs are events that are happening around us, which shape or change the way society runs. At a local level, something a simple as a factory closure can have a major effect on a small community, as many people may have been reliant on the factory for employment. At a national level, an election can change how the UK is run, and at an international level, a war can often involve many countries and bring about major changes to nations.

We can also divide the issues we look at into economic, political and social. An economic issue is to do with how people or a country make and spend money. A political issue is one which looks at how countries are run and how countries interact with one another. A social issue is one which concerns people's emotional and health needs.

Show your understanding

1. Explain what is meant by the following terms:
   Local
   National
   International

2. Take a full page in your jotter. Create a table like the one below. In each column, list three events which have affected you, your family, or local or national citizens. Explain what changes these events have caused.

Local	National	International
	For example, 2010 General Election = change of government. This led to many changes, for example, the new government increased the tax we pay on consumer goods (VAT). This makes everyone's shopping more expensive.	

3. Decide whether the following issues are social, economic or political:
   * Jobs
   * Healthcare provision
   * War
   * Income
   * Elections
   * Dictatorship
   * Crime
   * Debt
   * Education

Skills for life!

Here we will focus on the skills you will learn in Modern Studies – the things you will get better at as we go through the book. Keep your skills work somewhere safe – the back of your jotter is a good idea. These skills are not simply subject skills but skills you will need throughout school and in life. Who says Modern Studies is not important?

Collect a skill

Increase your word power!

This skill is all about words. You will come across many words in this book which you may not have read or heard before. Learning how to spell them and what they mean will **increase your word power** and really help you to communicate with other people.

When you find a word in **bold** or in a vocabulary bubble, or an idea you do not understand, record it in a vocabulary list. Explain its meaning in words and/or pictures. Ask your teacher or use a dictionary or encyclopaedia to help you understand the meaning.

Remind yourself to do this for all the chapters in the book to **boost your skill level!**

2 What is the news?

What are we exploring?

By the end of this section you should be able to:

▶ Explain the purpose of the media
▶ Explain why a free media is important

There are many ways that we can find out about what is happening in the world around us. We can read a daily newspaper, watch a television news programme or listen to a news bulletin on the radio. Most of the major television and radio stations in the UK have their own news programmes. These will tell us about world and national events. Most local television stations, radio stations and newspapers will also tell you about the things that are happening in your area. Many people access information about what is happening in the world on the Internet. We sometimes refer to 'the news' as **current affairs**.

Television, newspapers, radio stations and the Internet are collectively known as the media. All countries have a system of media and this is usually the main way for citizens to access information about the government and what is happening in the world around them. Most **democratic countries** have a free media. This means that the government does not interfere too much in what news stories are published.

Most people access the media in many forms

❓ Bore your friends...

12,681,472 people in the UK buy a newspaper every day.

⚙ Activate your brain cells

What types of media do you regularly use? Where do you get your news from? In what ways would your life be different if you did not have any access to the media?

In the UK, different television channels or newspapers have the freedom to present stories in slightly different ways. Many newspapers have a political bias. This means they support a particular political party and this often comes across in their stories. For example, one newspaper might write a story about how good a job the Prime Minister is doing of leading the country and another might write a story about how badly he is doing. This is important as it allows citizens to see many different viewpoints on issues. It is up to the citizens of the country to decide what story they agree with, and they are free to express their own opinions without getting in trouble with the government. However, the media is not allowed to publish lies. If they do they would be breaking the law and may have to go to court, where they may face a serious punishment. When a country has a free media, it is sometimes called having freedom of press.

In many non-democratic countries there is no freedom of press. This can help the government of a country keep control of power. For example, in China the government likes to keep tight control over what stories are published and how they are told. Many individuals who do not agree with these strict controls try to get around them by publishing blogs or 'illegal' newspapers. They think that the government is trying hide things from its citizens which could make them dislike the government. The Chinese government often jails journalists who publish stories that they do not want people to know or do not agree with. Up to 34 journalists are thought to be jailed at present in China for their work, and some journalists in the past have even received the death penalty for their publications in China.

democratic countries: countries that allow their citizens to vote and influence decision-making.

Show your understanding

1. What is the media?
2. What does it mean if a country has a free media?
3. Why is it important to have a free media?
4. Even if a country has a free media, what are journalists not allowed to do?
5. Why does the Chinese government not allow freedom of press?

Stretch yourself

The clue is in the name!
Keep a news diary. Write down a short story in the back of your jotter each week which gives the details of one local, national or world event which is happening. At the end of the year you will be able to review the main news stories that have happened.

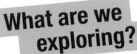

What is digital activism?

By the end of this section you should be able to:

▶ Provide evidence that the Internet is becoming more important worldwide

▶ Explain what is mean by digital activism

▶ Identify potential problems of increased Internet access

The Internet is becoming increasingly important as a source of information and method of communication within our global society. It is estimated that 59% of European citizens have access to the Internet. Even in poorer countries, the number of people who have access to the Internet has grown dramatically as Internet access has become cheaper. On the African continent, the number of people accessing the Internet has grown 22 times since the year 2000. Although it is not that common for African citizens to have a home computer, there are huge numbers of people going online at Internet cafes and via mobile phones.

Many people on the African continent now have access to the Internet

The growth in affordable Internet access has led to the Internet becoming one of the main methods of social communication. One of the biggest areas of growth has been the use of social networking websites such as Facebook and Twitter, particularly amongst young people. Their importance as a communication tool has grown so much that many politicians regularly use Facebook or Twitter as a means of connecting with younger voters. The US government has recently announced that it will publish warnings of terrorist threats through Facebook and Twitter, as it considers these to be more effective at reaching its population than existing methods. Even the Queen now has a Facebook page in order to increase her profile worldwide.

? Bore your friends...

As of April 2011, there are an estimated 312,693,296 websites on the Internet. Several million new sites are added each month.

Source: Netcraft.com

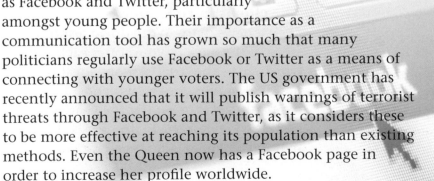

Activate your brain cells

What do you use the Internet for? Make a list of all the reasons your class uses the Internet.

What is digital activism?

Social networking websites and mobile phones have more recently played an important role in social mobilisation. This is often referred to as digital activism. In 2010, using Facebook and Twitter, students managed to organise protests in London against government proposals to raise tuition fees in England and Wales. However, this increase in technology can also be misused. A minority of more extreme student protestors used the social networking technology on the day to quickly organise violent protests at the Conservative Party headquarters in London. On a more serious scale, it is acknowledged that this increase in technology also makes it easier for potential terrorists to organise themselves.

European and US governments generally view digital activism as a positive use of Internet technology. The recent uprisings against oppressive governments in North African countries, such as Tunisia, Egypt and Libya, have been linked to an increase in access to social networking technology. In the past, it has always been difficult for citizens of these countries to organise a protest without the government finding out about it and stopping it. Citizens have been using the Internet, texting and mobile phone videos to rally people together and show the rest of the world how oppressive their government can be. This type of communication is very difficult for a government to control. The US government has agreed to further support the work of digital activists in non-democratic countries by providing $30 million to help create web domains that cannot easily be blocked by their own governments.

Stretch yourself

Survey your classmates to find out if they used the Internet yesterday and what they used it for. Choose a method to present your findings, for example:

- a bar graph
- a pictogram
- a pie chart
- a table.

Show your understanding

1. What evidence is there that the Internet is becoming an important communication tool within our world?
2. Why is the Internet becoming more widely used?
3. What evidence is there that politicians and national governments consider social networking sites a good way to communicate with people?
4. What is digital activism? Give an example to support your answer.
5. How can social networking technology be misused? Give an example to support your answer.
6. How did social networking technology help the uprisings in North Africa?

4 What is journalism?

What are we exploring?

By the end of this section you should be able to:

▶ Describe the work of a journalist
▶ Identify the qualities and skills that a good journalist should have
▶ Understand why some journalists choose to work in dangerous places

Every news story which you read in a newspaper, magazine or online or watch on the television has been researched and prepared by a journalist. Journalists are responsible for collecting information and writing, editing and presenting news stories or news articles for newspapers and magazines. Journalists do not report just on current affairs. Some might specialise in areas such as sport or entertainment. Anna Wintour became very famous and influential as the editor of the fashion magazine *Vogue*. It can be a very varied job depending on what aspect of society a journalist covers. No matter what area journalists cover, they all need to have the same skills and qualities to carry out their work effectively.

Journalists play a very important role in society in making sure citizens have access to information about what is going on in the world. For this reason, it is important that journalists act responsibly by making sure the information which they present to us is always truthful and accurate. Journalists are often very powerful because the work they publish can influence the opinions of huge sections of society about an issue, individual, organisation or government.

Anna Wintour, editor of American *Vogue* magazine

What skills and qualities should a journalist have?

- Be observant.
- Have good communication skills (talking and listening).
- Have the ability to record information accurately.
- Have the ability to write well, and always check spelling and grammar.
- Be confident.
- Always act responsibly.

Can you think why each of these qualities/ skills are important for a journalist? When will they be used?

Why do some journalists choose to work in very dangerous places?

Many journalists choose to work in very dangerous situations, such as war zones, because they believe it is important that world citizens have information about what is happening there. Many journalists, such as the BBC's John Simpson, have made a career out of reporting from countries experiencing conflict. John Simpson dodged bullets fired from Chinese government forces during the pro-democracy protests in Tiananmen Square in Beijing in 1989. Since then, he has reported from Iraq during the 1991 Gulf War, avoided capture from government forces in Zimbabwe while reporting on the dictator Mugabe, and most recently has travelled with rebel forces in Libya in 2011 during the anti-government uprisings.

A journalist in body armour reporting from a conflict zone

Working as a journalist in a conflict zone takes a special type of person. As well as being physically fit, they often need to be emotionally strong to cope with some of the terrible scenes they may encounter along with the reality that they may be hurt or taken hostage. In many cases, they rely on local help to keep them safe, and usually have access to a flak jacket, protective helmet, emergency funds and extra documentation such as spare passports. Most journalists in war zones never carry a weapon as they usually want to maintain their status of being neutral. In the last 20 years, over 800 journalists worldwide have lost their lives while working.

Show your understanding

1. What do journalists do?
2. Why is the work of a journalist important?
3. Why do some journalists choose to work in dangerous places?
4. What additional qualities and preparations does a journalist who is working in a conflict zone need to make?
5. Why would carrying a weapon in a conflict zone place a journalist at more risk?

Collect a skill

Imagine

Using your imagination is an important skill to develop for life. It helps you to think your way out of your environment and call upon your previous knowledge.

Use your imagination to write a story about a day in the life of a journalist in a conflict zone.

5 How do I write a news report?

By the end of this section you should be able to:

▶ Gather information
▶ Present the information in your own words as a news report

One way to show that you understand the events that are happening around you in society is to be able to present the information back to other people. One way you can do this is by writing your own news report. You can do this by creating a newspaper front page, a radio broadcast or a news programme. When reporting a news story, there are some key aspects to remember.

Gathering information: You need a lot of information to write a news report. You must make sure that all of the facts you use are accurate. You can gather information from existing news sources to help you with your report. Try to make sure your sources of information are reliable (can be trusted). TIP: you can print off news stories from online news sites to help you.

Writing in your own words: You must make sure that all of the information, except direct eyewitness accounts, has been put into your own words. Copying work from the work of others is known as plagiarism.

Structure: News reports are usually not overly long, but they must still get all of the relevant information across. It might help if you break down your news story into short paragraphs. This will make it easier to lay out in a newspaper style, or read out if you are preparing a broadcast. TIP: Look at a newspaper or watch/listen to a newsbroadcast to get ideas about how to lay your story out.

Collect a skill

Gathering information

One key skill in Modern Studies, as well as in many other subjects, is to be able to research a topic and record it accurately. This is called gathering information. You will need to gather information on your chosen news story. If it is a local story, you may need to look at local news reports and could even interview local people. The Internet is a good source of information, but you must try to use only what you know to be reliable sources. Most of the main national newspapers or television stations are reliable sources of information.

It is sometimes easier to record data by using bullet-point notes. Make sure you note down accurately any facts or figures that are relevant to your story. Try to use at least three different sources of information for your news story.

Make a careful note of each of your sources (e.g. the website or newspaper, as well as the author and date it was written if available). You may be asked for these later by your teacher. If you are using an eyewitness account, you must include within your presentation information on who the eyewitness is and what their connection is to your story.

Let's think about our news reports for a minute. What could you prepare your news report on?

Make a list with a friend of a selection of news stories you could base your report on.

Identify possible sources of information for your news report.

Decide how you are going to present your news report.

Here is a checklist of additional things you need to consider about your news broadcast.

Big news from the classroom

Newspaper report

You should have:

1. a large piece of paper, preferably A3 size

2. a newspaper name

3. a 'catchy' headline to attract readers

4. a main story, with accurate details about the event you are describing

5. an eyewitness account (optional)

6. text written in columns

7. an illustration (with captions) to accompany your story.

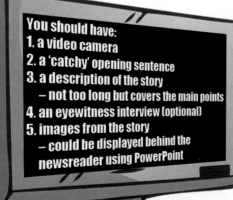

You should have:
1. a video camera
2. a 'catchy' opening sentence
3. a description of the story
   – not too long but covers the main points
4. an eyewitness interview (optional)
5. images from the story
   – could be displayed behind the newsreader using PowerPoint

You should have:
1. a recording device, e.g. an MP3 recorder
2. a 'catchy' opening sentence
3. a description of the story
   – not too long but covers the main points
4. an eyewitness interview (optional)
5. a jingle for your programme (optional)

A television news broadcast   A radio broadcast

6 Why do we have rules and laws?

What are we exploring?

By the end of this section you should be able to:

▶ Explain the difference between a rule and a law
▶ Understand why rules and laws are important in our society

Rules and laws are an important part of our society. They exist to make sure that society operates in an orderly way and individuals' rights are protected. Without rules and laws, society would be chaotic and there would be times when you would not know what to do. Rules are usually made by individuals and organisations, and **enforced** by those organisations. Laws are made by the government. They are usually enforced by the police or other government **institutions**.

Most people are happy to follow rules and laws as they understand that they protect their rights and keep everybody safe. You usually face certain consequences if you break a rule or a law. These are important as they **deter** against breaking a particular rule or law.

Even within school we all follow lots of rules. Most schools have a code of conduct to help students know what they should and should not do. Individual teachers may have additional rules that they want you to follow. These exist to make sure that classes are orderly and everyone has the opportunity to learn and remain safe.

Rules and laws sometimes change. A change of rule is usually decided upon by the individual or organisation who created it. They may consult those that the rule affects about the change, but they do not always have to. For example, if there was to be a major change in the rules for football, it would normally need to be agreed on by FIFA (International Federation of Association Football), which is the international governing body for the game. However, if

enforce: make sure that people obey
institutions: organisations that work for a particular part of society, e.g. the government

deter: put people off

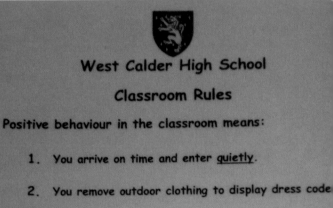

West Calder High School

Classroom Rules

Positive behaviour in the classroom means:

1. You arrive on time and enter <u>quietly</u>.

2. You remove outdoor clothing to display dress code

3. You <u>quickly</u> and <u>quietly</u> get ready for the lesson.

Most schools have a set of rules

Activate your brain cells!

Identify a rule which you would change from your school's code of conduct. Explain how and why you would change it.

Bill: a proposed law

? Bore your friends...

It is illegal to die in the Houses of Parliament.

someone proposes a change of law, it must be agreed on by parliament. The proposal would be submitted as a **Bill**. A majority of parliament (over 50%) must vote in favour of the Bill before it can become a law.

The Scottish Parliament has the power to make its own laws about certain issues. In 2009, the Scottish Government successfully persuaded a majority of Members of the Scottish Parliament (MSPs) to vote in favour of a law that changed the hours that shops could sell alcohol. This was an attempt to reduce the amount of underage and binge drinking by reducing the number of hours in which alcohol would be available to buy. Now shops in Scotland can only sell alcohol between the hours of 10 a.m. and 10 p.m.

However, the SNP government tried to take this further in 2010 by introducing a Bill which proposed minimum pricing of alcohol. Their argument was that it would further discourage underage and binge

Shops must follow strict rules about when they can sell alcohol

drinking by making alcohol much more expensive to obtain. However, this was not supported by a majority of MSPs in parliament, and the Bill was defeated by 76 votes to 49. This shows us that not all Bills receive the amount of support they require to become a law.

Show your understanding

1. What is the difference between a rule and a law?
2. Why do most people follow rules and laws?
3. What are the consequences of breaking rules and laws?
4. How does the government change laws?
5. Pick three rules from your school's code of conduct. Explain why each of these rules is important, and what the consequences would be of breaking them.

Collect a skill

Identifying exaggeration

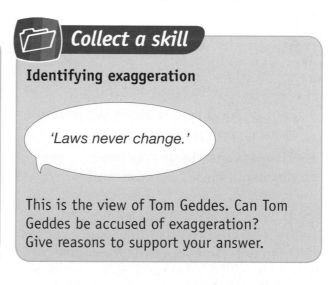

'Laws never change.'

This is the view of Tom Geddes. Can Tom Geddes be accused of exaggeration? Give reasons to support your answer.

REVIEW

Make a poster explaining a law that exists in either Scotland or the entire UK. Your poster should include the law itself, a suitable illustration and a explanation of why it is important that people follow the law.

7 Who enforces the law in the UK?

What are we exploring?

By the end of this section you should be able to:

▶ Identify the groups, other than the police, who enforce the law

▶ Describe the methods they use to enforce the law

Most people willingly follow the law as they understand that it there to protect their rights and ensure the safety of all. However, we still have several organisations which enforce the law. The most important law enforcement organisation in the UK is the police. They have a responsibility to prevent crimes from taking place, to protect and reassure the community and to detect and investigate criminals.

However, local councils usually have several other officials who enforce the law, such as environmental wardens, traffic wardens and planning officials. These officials specialise in enforcing the law in specific areas. However, when faced with difficult situations, these officials may also turn to the police to help them enforce the law because they usually do not have the right to detain or search suspects, or use any type of physical force.

Activate your brain cells!

Can you think of what methods the police use to enforce the law? Try to create a list with a friend.

Environmental wardens

Duties:

- Investigate environmental crime (such as littering and dog fouling).
- Educate local people about the impact of local environmental crime.

Methods: Councils usually have environmental wardens constantly patrolling local areas to deter people from breaking environmental laws. In many local council areas they are permitted to issue spot fines for people caught breaking local laws, such as allowing their dog to foul and not picking up after it. Environmental wardens are responsible for investigating reports of environmental crime, such as graffiti, dumping litter or creating unacceptable levels of noise at **antisocial** hours. They sometimes have the power to force private building owners to tidy up their property if it poses a risk to public health.

Environmental warden at work

Bore your friends...

Illegal dumping costs local councils across the UK almost £1 million per week to clear up.

14

Traffic wardens

Duties:

- Ensure that people do not park illegally.
- Ensure that parking meters work correctly.
- Direct traffic in the event of broken traffic lights/systems.
- Look out for stolen vehicles and out-of-date tax discs.

Methods: Traffic wardens usually patrol on foot and check that vehicles are not parked illegally or have paid to park in controlled parking zones. They have the power to issue on-the-spot fines if a vehicle is parked illegally. If a vehicle is parked dangerously or is obstructing traffic, they can order it to be removed and impounded. The owner usually has to pay a substantial fine to have the vehicle returned.

Traffic wardens are responsible for enforcing local parking restrictions

Planning officers

Duties:

- Ensure that new buildings meet current planning regulations.
- Conserve old buildings and sites of special interest.

Methods: Planning officers usually work with local citizens, architects and builders to ensure than any new buildings or planned extensions meet current planning laws and will fit in with the existing buildings in the area. They have the power to refuse planning permission or suggest amendments if they do not. They can even demand that a construction project that is already completed, but does not meet building regulations, is upgraded or knocked down. They often have the power to force owners of buildings to make essential repairs if their building is considered to be in a dangerous state.

Stretch yourself

Using your local council website, research the work of either environmental wardens, traffic wardens or planning officers in your local area. Write a short report on the work that they do.

Show your understanding

1. Who is the most important law enforcement organisation in the UK? Explain your answer.
2. Who else has organisations that can enforce the law?
3. Pick one of the local council organisations that enforce the law. Complete the following information about it using bullet points:
   Title
   Duties
   Powers to enforce

⑧ What role do the courts play?

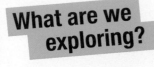

What are we exploring?

By the end of this section you should be able to:

▶ Describe the role of the courts in Scotland

▶ Explain the difference between Civil and Criminal Courts

▶ Identify what alternatives to court there are for children

A court is an institution set up by the government through which people settle disputes via a legal process. They listen to all of the arguments surrounding a case, decide whether or not a person is guilty of committing a crime and decide what the punishment should be. They also help people resolve private disputes in a peaceful way. Everybody in the UK has the right to have a fair trial. This means that they have the right to publicly put forward their version of events and defend themselves.

Scotland has always had a separate legal system from the UK and therefore also has a slightly different court system. In Scotland, a case can be heard at either a Civil Court or a Criminal Court.

One of Scotland's Sherriff Courts

High Court judge in gown

Civil Courts usually hear cases that involve private disputes. Examples of cases that a Civil Court would hear are divorce cases, land disputes and cases surrounding the debt or bankruptcy of an individual. The case will be heard by a sheriff, and he or she will make a decision about what the outcome of the case should be. The outcome is not always a punishment, for example, in a land dispute it can be as simple as making a decision about where a disputed boundary line between two properties exists.

Criminal Courts focus on whether or not an individual has committed a crime. In the case of minor offences, such as being drunk and disorderly or driving through a red traffic light, the case may be heard before a

Justice of the Peace Court. Trials for more serious crimes, such as being in possession of drugs, theft or assault, will be heard at a Sheriff Court. The most serious crimes, such as murder or rape, are heard at the High Court. Cases heard in both the Sheriff and High Court are usually conducted in front of a jury, and the jury will decide whether or not a person is guilty.

In Scotland, a jury is made up of 15 people aged between 18 and 70 years old. Anybody who is between these ages, on the electoral register and has lived in the UK for over 5 years may be called up for jury duty at any time. You must do jury duty if required, unless you have an exemption. Certain professions are **exempted** from jury duty, such as doctors, solicitors and politicians. It is the judge who decides what **sentence** a person who is found guilty should be given.

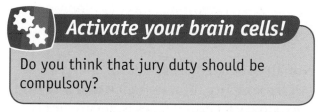

? Bore your friends...

A High Court Judge in Scotland always wears a white cloak with red crosses on it.

⚙ Activate your brain cells!

Do you think that jury duty should be compulsory?

exempted: you do not have to participate in a particular activity
sentence: the punishment a person convicted of a crime should receive

Children who commit crimes are usually sent to the Children's Hearing System rather than court, unless it is a very serious crime such as murder. Their case will be heard in front of three panel members who are volunteers. The Children's Hearing System is designed to be less intimidating for a young person than a court, and focuses on encouraging a person to change his or her behaviour rather than on punishment. The Children's Hearing System is also designed to protect children and hears cases in which children have been neglected by parents, persistently truanting from school, or involved in drugs or solvent abuse. They may refer the child to other agencies that can support him or her, for example a social worker, and in extreme cases it may be decided that it is in a child's best interests to be removed from the home.

🧩 Show your understanding

1. What is the purpose of a court?
2. What rights should a person have in a fair trial?
3. Name the three types of criminal court in Scotland, and explain the differences between them.
4. Explain who can be called for jury duty.
5. Why do you think some professions are exempt from jury duty? Explain using examples.
6. Why are children often referred to the Children's Hearing System if they have committed a crime?

9 What consequences do those convicted of a crime face?

What are we exploring?

By the end of this section you should be able to:
▶ Identify the aims of sentencing
▶ Describe different types of sentences given in Scotland
▶ Identify the advantages and problems of different types of sentencing

Not all convicted criminals are given a prison sentence. The sentence that a person convicted of a crime faces is dependent on many factors. These include the seriousness of their crime, whether they have any previous convictions, the motives behind their crime, if they have a drug habit and whether or not they pose a danger to the general public.

Judges will pass the sentence that he or she feels most appropriately meets the following aims:

- The person is punished for the crime.
- The individual concerned is deterred from committing the crime again.
- The individual is given an opportunity to rehabilitate.
- The public is protected from the person.

There are a number of options that a judge can use when passing sentence on an individual.

Prison

People are most often sent to prison if they have committed a serious crime, are a repeat offender or are considered to be a danger to the public. When an individual is sent to prison, they lose all of their freedom and have very restricted access to family and friends. The Scottish Government now discourages judges from awarding short prison sentences (6 months or less) because they believe that criminals have no opportunity to rehabilitate, and many come out having learned even worse behaviour from fellow prisoners. Some even describe prisons as 'universities of crime'.

Community Payback Orders

Community Payback Orders are now the preferred sentencing option used for low-level offenders. These come in many forms, such as:

- carrying out hours of unpaid work in the community
- having an enforced curfew of when they must not go outwith their home
- paying compensation to the victim of their crime
- reporting regularly to the police
- participating in drug or alcohol treatment programmes.

Many people are concerned that Community Payback Orders allow dangerous criminals to remain in the community, giving them the potential to carry out further crimes. However, the Scottish Government argues that Community Payback Orders provide many more opportunities for rehabilitation of the criminal, and allow them to repay the community somehow. They argue that they

18

Convicted criminals can be tracked by tagging devices

Fines are often awarded for traffic offences

can keep track of criminals through regular contact with local police forces and through methods such as compulsory electronic tagging of individuals.

Fines

Fines are usually awarded for less serious crimes. There are fixed fines awarded for particular offences, such as breaches of road traffic laws. Many people who are caught speeding while driving are given a fixed fine and points on their licence. Only if they continue to breach road traffic laws may they face court and a more serious penalty. Fines are also awarded in court as a punishment for all sorts of crimes. Often a person convicted of a crime is fined so that compensation money can be awarded to the victim of their crime. Fines punish a person financially by limiting the amount of money they have to spend. Many fines given are only a few hundred pounds, and many feel that this is not an adequate deterrent for offenders.

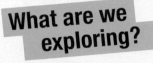

What is it like inside prison?

What are we exploring?

By the end of this section you should be able to:

▶ Describe what life inside prison is like

▶ Identify the problems prisoners may face upon release

▶ Create a mind map

The most severe sentence that can be awarded in the UK is a prison sentence. The current prison population in the UK is 83,000, including 8000 Scottish prisoners. The UK has the highest prison population per head of population in Western Europe, and many prisons in the UK are very overcrowded. Prison removes almost all of the freedom that an individual has. Here is a look at what life inside prison can be like for inmates in the UK.

Prison reception

All prisoners begin their sentence at reception. Every inmate is strip-searched to make sure that they are not bringing in any drugs, weapons or illegal items, such as phones. They must give up all their possessions, including clothes, and will be given prison-issue clothes to wear. They are seen by a member of medical staff who assesses their medical needs and mental state before being placed in a cell. A prisoner deemed to be in a poor mental state may be kept in an isolated cell for a short time.

Cells

The accommodation varies from prison to prison, but most prisoners will have to share a room with at least one other person. There will be a toilet in the room. Food and shower areas are a shared space. Prisoners are normally allowed televisions in their rooms, but they are not allowed mobile phones, games consoles or MP3 players. Many people do not agree that prisoners should be allowed televisions.

Activate your brain cells!

Do you think prisoners should be allowed to have televisions in their cells? Why do you think prisons usually allow prisoners to have televisions in their cells?

Education/rehabilitation/religion

Most prisoners serving 6 months or more have the opportunity to participate in a rehabilitation and education course. This can help them prepare for life outside prison once they are released. They may get support to quit a drug habit or with anger management. There are also usually opportunities for prisoners to get **vocational qualifications**. At Cornton Vale Women's Prison, many inmates manage to get beauty therapy or hairdressing qualifications. Some long-term inmates even complete degree courses. Most prisons have a multi-faith room where inmates of all religions can worship.

vocational qualifications: qualifications that prepare a person to do a particular job

Food

Prisons in the UK spend on average £1.87 per day per inmate on providing prison food. Prison kitchens are often partially staffed by inmates who have gained the trust of prison officers. Prisons now generally offer healthy options for food, and cater for special diets, but they still do not have a large budget to feed inmates.

Fitness

Most prisons have some kind of exercise space for inmates, and many organise sports and have a gym. This helps inmates keep physically fit and it has been found that sport and exercise can also be of psychological benefit to inmates. However, in some prisons which are understaffed, prisoners may only receive an hour of exercise time per day.

Contact with family/friends

Visits from family and friends are tightly controlled. Visitors must be searched before entry in case they try to bring in prohibited items. Visits are short and sometimes restricted to once a month. Prisoners are allowed to make phone calls and are allowed to send one letter per week. Some prisoners may earn the right to send a second letter, but they will have to pay for the stamp themselves. All letters sent and received are **censored** by prison staff.

censored: checked for inappropriate content

Show your understanding

1. What problems do prisons in the UK currently face?
2. Why are new prisoners searched and given new clothes upon their arrival at prison?
3. Why is it important that prisoners get access to rehabilitation and education during their time in prison?
4. What problems or challenges might prisoners face upon their release from prison?
5. Why are letters coming in and going out of prison censored?
6. Write a list of all of the freedoms that prisoners give up.

Collect a skill

Mind mapping!

Learning how to draw mind maps might help you in your school subjects. Mind mapping is a method you can use to help you organise your thoughts. In the middle of your page draw a circle and write 'Life inside prison' inside it. Now draw six lines coming out from the circle. It should look like the diagram in the example opposite. Use the text to help you write a small amount about each of the aspects of prison life, and add in some pictures.

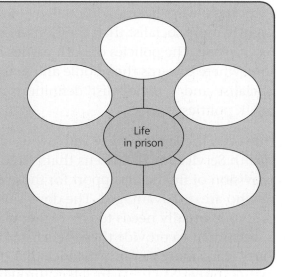

Life in prison

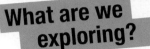

What is an ideology?

An ideology is how you think something should be run. Your head teacher will have an ideology about how your school should be run, and this will usually determine what rules you must follow when in school. Political parties all have ideologies about how they would run the country.

Some political parties believe that the government should provide for all people, for example, by providing benefits. This is known as a 'socialist' ideology. Other political parties believe that individuals should have the opportunity to make themselves rich by working hard, but should also be able to provide for their own needs. This is known as an 'individualist' ideology.

All political parties have an ideology, which determines their policies

policies: what a party promises to do if elected

In the UK, there are very few examples of extreme socialist or individualist political parties. The Labour Party has always been traditionally viewed as being slightly more socialist than the Conservative Party. In recent years, the policies of both parties have moved somewhere towards the middle and many feel that the 'socialist' and 'individualist' definitions no longer apply in UK politics.

However, the Labour Party still favours a strong National Health Service for all citizens that is free to use, and the provision of financial support for those on a low income or who are disadvantaged. The downside of this is that everyone usually needs to pay higher taxes to allow a government to provide these benefits. The Conservative Party leans more towards the idea that people should be mainly providing for themselves through working. Their **policies** tend not to be as individualist as the main US political parties, but they have made several cuts to benefits for people in the UK since they formed a

Some political parties, such as the Green Party, focus on a particular issue. In their case it is increasing the use of green energy

coalition government with the Liberal Democrats, in 2010. One example of this is their plan to stop child benefit in 2013 for families who have one parent earning over £43,000 per year. In the past, all families in the UK with children received child benefit to help them meet the extra costs of having a child.

Some political parties in the UK are formed with one particular main focus. For example, the Green Party is focused on improving the environment. Its main policies are about increasing our use of green energy in the UK (such as wind power) and forcing more people to recycle and reduce the amount of waste that they produce.

Activate your brain cells!

What kind of ideology do you have?
Write out the four statements that you agree with most.

> Everyone should be entitled to benefits such as free healthcare.

> People who earn less money should get help to make ends meet.

> People who earn more should not be punished for being successful by having to pay higher taxes.

> Rich people should pay more tax to help those who are less fortunate.

> Everyone in the UK has an equal opportunity to become successful; it is up to them to work hard to make it happen.

> The government has a responsibility to help the elderly make ends meet by providing them with a pension.

> It is fair that if you have the money to pay for private healthcare, or a private education for your children, you have the opportunity to do so.

> People should expect to provide for their retirement by saving money while they are working.

With a partner, decide if each statement is from a socialist or a individualist ideology.
Do you think you have more of a socialist or individualist ideology?

Show your understanding

1. What is an ideology?
2. What do 'socialist' political parties believe?
3. What do 'individualist' political parties believe?
4. Are you more socialist or individualist? Give a reason for your answer.

Stretch yourself

Research a political party other than Labour or Conservative. Identify what their main policies are and decide what type of ideology they have.

12 What is the difference between capitalism and communism?

By the end of this section you should be able to:
▶ Describe what is meant by capitalism
▶ Describe what is meant by communism

The UK is often described as having a capitalist **economy**. This means that the government interferes very little in how businesses are run within the country, and how they make money. People who live in a country with a capitalist economy are generally free to get a job doing whatever they want, as long as they are not doing something illegal. They are even free to start their own business. The most successful people can become very wealthy. Capitalism gives people much more freedom and choice than communism.

Despite operating as a capitalist economy, the UK still provides for its citizens in many ways. Everyone is entitled to use the National Health Service for free, to receive a state pension when they retire and to have access to many financial benefits if they live on a low income or they are unable to work because they are made redundant, become sick or are disabled. Many would therefore describe the UK as still having many strong socialist elements.

economy: how a country makes and spends money

The USA is even more of a capitalist economy than the UK. It does not provide so many benefits for its citizens. Everyone in the USA must pay for his or her own healthcare. However, some argue that this allows them to access better quality treatment because patients can also often choose which hospital and sometimes even which doctors treat them. However, you can only get access to the best healthcare in the USA if you are rich. Access to welfare benefits is very limited, with only the very poorest getting some financial assistance with things such as very basic healthcare.

The UK government provides a free national health service for its citizens

NHS
Lothian

Welcome to
**St. John's Hospital
Livingston**

What is communism?

Communism is a political and economic system of government that focuses on trying to make everyone equal. Communist governments try to achieve this by controlling every aspect of their citizens' lives. They often own all industry, business and property so that they can redistribute this to everyone fairly. This means that communist governments usually choose what jobs people do and how much they earn, as well all aspects of housing, healthcare and education.

Activate your brain cells!

What are the good and bad things about capitalism? Create a list with a friend.

There are very few communist countries left around the world, following the collapse of the Soviet Union in the early 1990s. Many people think that communism is a good idea in principle.

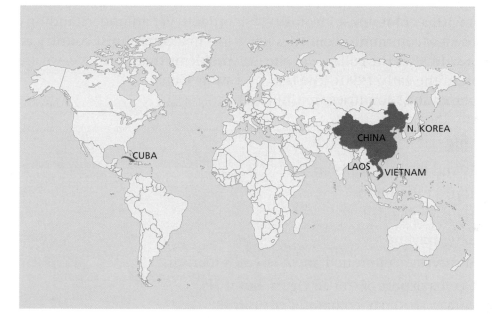

Show your understanding

1. What relationship does the government have with businesses in a capitalist economy?
2. What freedoms do people living in a capitalist economy usually have?
3. What problems can people living in a capitalist economy face? Give examples to support your answer.
4. What is communism?
5. How do communist governments try to make sure everyone is equal?

13 What is it like to live in a communist country?

By the end of this section you should be able to:

▶ Describe what led to Cuba becoming a communist country

▶ Describe what happened to Cubans who disagreed with communism

A communist country is one that has a government with a communist ideology. There are very few communist countries left around the world after the collapse of the Soviet Union in the early 1990s. The last remaining communist countries are China, Cuba, Laos, North Korea and Vietnam. In order to get an understanding of that life is like in a communist country and the problems that they face, we are going to study Cuba.

Cuba fact file

- Largest island in the Caribbean Sea.
- Population: 11.9 million.
- Main language: Spanish.
- Capital city: Havana.
- Main industry: agriculture and, more recently, tourism.
- Famous for its export of Cuban cigars, but it also exports Sugar, shellfish, coffee and citrus fruit.

A communist government was implemented in Cuba in 1959, after a successful armed revolution overthrew the previous **dictatorship**. The revolution was led by the country's first communist leader, Fidel Castro. Fidel Castro remained the leader of Cuba's communist government for almost 40 years, until he stood down because of ill health in 2008. Fidel was replaced by his brother and former defence minister, Raúl.

Until Castro's communist regime took control in 1959, there was evidence of huge inequalities between the rich and the poor living in Cuba. His aim was to redistribute property and wealth in order to create a more equal society. However, in order to do this his government had to use some fairly severe methods, such as taking all private property off the wealthy and making it the property of the government. All private businesses were either closed down or **nationalised**, and many people who had previously been quite wealthy soon found that they owned very little.

dictatorship: a country ruled by one individual with no democratic elections

nationalised: taken under control by the government

Did everybody agree with Castro's changes?

Many people did not agree with the communist revolution in Cuba, particularly those who had any kind of wealth. Castro dealt with anybody who resisted his changes by imprisoning them. As a consequence of this, Cuba has an enormous prison system despite the relatively small size of the population. There are 70 prisons within the country and over 200 labour camps. Many Cuban citizens fled the country to seek **refuge** in the USA. Many have been so desperate to escape the **oppression** they face in Cuba that they have risked their lives to make the 90-mile journey across dangerous seas to the USA in homemade rafts and tyre inner tubes.

The main groups who left Cuba, once the communist regime began, were skilled professionals such as engineers and medical staff. They realised that they would never be able to have the standard of living or freedom that they had been used to under the new regime.

About 10% of Cubans now live in the USA, and as a result of their high level of experience and qualifications, they have been particularly successful in jobs such as banking and medicine. Their departure caused a huge problem for Castro because he lost many talented individuals who had the skills he was relying upon to make his country strong and successful.

Fidel Castro

Many are so desperate to flee that they use makeshift rafts

refuge: shelter from a dangerous individual or government
oppression: having your freedom severely restricted

Show your understanding

1. Which are the last remaining countries with a communist government?
2. Why did Castro want to start a communist government in Cuba?
3. What happened to people who owned property?
4. What happened to people who disagreed with the communist government?
5. Who were the main people to leave Cuba? Why did this cause a problem for Castro?

? Bore your friends...

Fidel Castro reportedly survived over 600 assassination attempts during his leadership.

Explore further

The US military has a famous military base in eastern Cuba called Guantanamo Bay. What facts can you find out about this military base?

14 What is it like to live in a communist country? (cont.)

What are we exploring?

By the end of this section you should be able to:
▶ Identify the benefits that communism has brought to many Cubans
▶ Describe the recent changes to the Cuban economy

Has communism brought any benefits to Cubans?

In many respects communism has been successful in Cuba. The gap between the rich and the poor has decreased greatly. Areas of society such as education, healthcare and welfare benefits have been made accessible to all and are generally considered to be of a high standard. Improving healthcare was a particular focus for the Cuban government. It has built up a highly regarded healthcare system despite losing over half of the trained medical staff in the country, who fled at the beginning of the communist regime. Cuba has had a vaccination programme in place since the 1960s to combat the world's killer diseases. It has now eradicated illnesses such as tetanus, malaria, tuberculosis and polio. Life expectancy is similar to that in Scotland, at 77 years for men and 81 years for women.

Education is also of a high standard. Cuba's literacy rate has risen over 30% since communism began to 99.8%, which again is the same as a Scotland. Education is highly valued and Cuba has 100% school attendance.

But at what cost?

The evidence suggests that Cubans are perhaps much better off than they were before, but at a price. The main cost has been people's freedom. Cuba, like most communist countries, has tried to guarantee that everyone is equal by tightly controlling society. Almost everything (property, industry, businesses) is owned by the government, and they decide who gets what. They even decide where people live. All parts of the media are owned by the government, and it is illegal for most people to access the Internet.

The Cuban government is very frightened that any more of its skilled workforce will leave in search of greater freedom and wealth, so all citizens must obtain permission to change job. Very few get permission to leave the country, and if they do they have many restrictions placed upon them to ensure that they return.

Cuba was also very reliant on the former Soviet Union (which Russia used to be part of) to subsidise them with imports of food and oil. When communism ended there, Cuba lost a valuable source of income and basic goods. This led to a period of poverty during the 1990s which the country is still struggling to recover from.

Changes to the Cuban economy

Like many of the remaining communist countries, Cuba has been forced to consider new ways to improve its economy. It has allowed many foreign companies to build luxury tourist resorts along its beautiful beaches in order to bring much needed income into the country. At first, foreign tourists who visited these resorts were not allowed to visit other parts of Cuba, but more recently they have been allowed to take tightly controlled tours around the country.

The new leader, Raúl Castro, has also allowed some private companies to open. He realised it was no longer possible to guarantee employment for everyone in government-owned businesses. He has also been working on improving Cuba's relationship with the US government since Obama became president. The USA had previously banned US citizens from travelling to or spending money in Cuba.

Cuba has boosted its economy with tourism

Show your understanding

1. Copy the table below and list the arguments for and against communism in Cuba.

Arguments for	Arguments against

2. Give two pieces of evidence that show that communism has brought some benefits to Cubans.
3. How did the collapse of the Soviet Union affect Cuba?
4. Why has the Cuban government allowed foreign companies to build tourist resorts in Cuba?
5. How is the new leader, Raúl Castro, opening up Cuba?

REVIEW

Using the last three chapters in the book, write a short report about whether or not you would like to live in a communist country. You must explain what communism means and examine both the advantages and disadvantages before coming to a conclusion.

How can I influence how the country is run?

The UK is a democratic country. Democracy is a political system that allows everyone to have a say in how their country is run. The UK system of government is known as a representative democracy. This means that citizens elect people to put their views forward and vote on their behalf on decisions made at the various levels of government in the UK. It would be impossible for everyone in the UK to directly have a say in the running of the country. If each person living in the UK had the opportunity to speak for 1 minute, it would take 118 years to get through everybody!

Everyone in Scotland has a representative at four different levels. These are:

- Local Council – Local Councillors
- Scottish Parliament – Members of the Scottish Parliament (MSPs)
- UK Parliament – Members of Parliament (MPs)
- European Parliament – Members of the European Parliament (MEPs).

Activate your brain cells!

Do you know who represents you? Use the Internet to find out who your local councillors, MSPs, MPs and MEPs are.

The people of Scotland have the opportunity to vote in elections at all levels, providing they are on the **electoral register.**

electoral register: a list of everyone who is allowed to vote

Your name is not automatically placed on the electoral register. You must apply to go onto the electoral register and can do this once you turn 16 years old. However, you will not actually be able to vote until you are 18 years old. It is easy to register as most households receive a freepost form at least once a year to allow them to update the people living in the household who wish to be on the electoral register. It can take 2 or 3 weeks to process your voter registration, so it is important that you register to vote as soon as you are old enough. This will ensure that you do not miss out on the opportunity to vote, as sometimes elections can be held earlier than expected. It is also important that you change your details on the electoral register if you move house, as you must be registered in the **constituency** you live within to be eligible to vote. The electoral register is important as it prevents people from voting twice, or voting when they are not permitted to do so.

constituency: the area that a representative will speak on behalf of in Parliament

Is every adult in the UK entitled to vote in a General Election?

The simple answer is no. Even if you are on the electoral register, you will be not be permitted to vote in a UK General Election if any of the following apply:

- You are under 18 years old.
- You are not a British citizen.
- You have a severe mental illness which prevents you from understanding the voting procedure.
- You are a member of the House of Lords.
- You are a prisoner (although this is likely to change as it has been declared against European Union [EU] human rights legislation).

An electoral registration form

In local council elections, Scottish Parliament and European Parliament elections, *all* EU citizens are permitted to vote.

It is important that people use their right to vote. Voting gives you the opportunity to voice your opinion on how the local area or country should be run. In many countries around the world, citizens do not have the same opportunities to participate in free and fair elections. Many people risk their lives to vote, and in many countries, such as parts of North Africa and the Middle East, people are fighting to have the opportunity to have more say in the running of their country. If you do not vote, you do not have a right to complain about any government decisions, as you have made no attempt to change things.

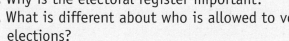

Show your understanding

1. What is a representative democracy?
2. What are the four levels that people in Scotland are represented at?
3. Why is the electoral register important?
4. What is different about who is allowed to vote in a UK General Election and all other elections?
5. Why is it important you use your right to vote?

REVIEW

Make a leaflet or a PowerPoint presentation encouraging people to register to vote. You can explain how they can do this and why it is important that they use their right to vote.

16 Why were the results of 2010 General Election unusual?

What are we exploring?

By the end of this section you should be able to:

▶ Explain the advantages and disadvantages of the first-past-the-post system

▶ Understand why the 2010 General Election produced unusual results

▶ Use data to create a pie chart

The **electoral system** used in the UK General Election is called 'first-past-the-post'. It is popular with many voters because it is easy to understand. The UK is divided up into 650 constituencies. Voters only vote for a candidate to represent them in the constituency they live in. They do this by placing an 'X' mark against the name of the candidate they wish to win on their ballot paper. The candidate who wins the most votes in that constituency, even if just by one vote, wins the seat in parliament. Some people view this system as being very unfair as it favours the Conservative and Labour parties in the UK. Other parties, such as the Liberal Democrat Party, are disadvantaged as they end up with far fewer seats overall because they often come second or third in constituencies, even though they may win a significant proportion of the overall vote.

All parties want to try and win a **majority** of seats in parliament because they need 50% of the votes to pass any new legislation. In the 2010 UK General Election, no party managed to win a majority of seats. This is sometimes called a 'hung parliament'. The Conservative Party won the most seats in the election, but they were 19 seats short of winning a majority in parliament. This is very unusual in a first-past-the-post election system, because the winning party usually achieves enough seats in parliament to have a strong majority government.

electoral system: a voting system

majority: over 50%

Table 16.1 2010 General Election results (326 seats needed for a majority)

Party	Number of seats	% of seats	% of vote
Conservative	307	47	36
Labour	258	40	29
Liberal Democrat	57	9	23
Other	28	4	12

Percentages are rounded to the nearest whole number.

A coalition is when two parties join together to achieve a majority of votes in parliament in order to pass legislation. Most parties will only agree to be part of a coalition if they get they get to influence policies. This can sometimes lead to watered-down laws, or parties voting for laws with which they do not really agree.

policies: what a party promises to do if elected

Activate your brain cells!

Think about why some people may think the results of the 2010 General Election are very unfair. Explain this to a friend (hint: compare the percentage of seats that each party won with the percentage of votes that each party received).

The Conservative Party was left with two options. It could operate either as a minority government or as a coalition. A minority government is when the party with the most seats forms a government, even though it does not have a majority. It must try and negotiate Bill by Bill with Members of Parliament (MPs) from other parties to pass legislation. It can be quite difficult at times to get the number of vote required to pass a law, especially if you have to persuade 19 MPs from other parties to vote for your **policies**. The Conservative government chose to join up with the Liberal Democrat Party to form a coalition.

The Conservative/Liberal Democrat government is the first formal coalition in the UK Parliament since World War Two. It has had a rocky start, and the Liberal Democrats have been heavily criticised for voting directly against some of their election promises, such as their policy to not increase tuition fees for students in England and Wales. Many people believe that the coalition will not last a full term (up to 5 years). A **referendum** was held in 2011 to see if British citizens wanted to change the voting system from first-past-the-post to a proportional electoral system. A proportional representation system would make coalition governments the norm in the UK, as it makes it very difficult for one party to win an overall majority. However, 68% of the population voted to keep the current first-past-the-post voting system.

referendum: when people vote directly on an issue

Show your understanding

1. What are two advantages of the first-past-the-post electoral system?
2. What is a disadvantage of a first-past-the-post electoral system?
3. What is a 'hung parliament'?
4. Why were the 2010 General Election results unusual?
5. What problems do coalition governments often face?

Collect a skill

Create a pie chart.

Being able to present data in another format is a useful skill and something you may have done in maths or other subjects. Use the data in Table 16.1 to create a pie chart showing the percentage of votes that each party won, and another showing the percentage of seats that each party won. Make sure you include a title and key showing what each segment represents.

17 How does my Member of Parliament represent me?

By the end of this section you should be able to:

▶ Describe the work of a Member of Parliament

▶ Identify the pressures that Members of Parliament face

Members of Parliament (MPs) are elected by their constituents in a General Election once every 5 years. MPs have a very important role to play in representing their constituents. If they are in the party which is in government, they are expected to help their party push forward its policies by voting in favour of any legislation which is proposed. If they are in an **opposition** party, it is their responsibility to scrutinise the work of the government and make sure they are representing the people. They have many ways of doing this.

opposition: a party that is not in government

Members of Parliament must divide their time between their constituency and the UK Parliament in London to carry out their work.

Work in their constituency

Members of Parliament use the time spent in their constituency to meet with constituents. They often hold surgeries in several locations across their constituency, in places such as local libraries or community centres, to allow constituents to discuss problems with them.

They also have a constituency office and a website through which they can be contacted. Most MPs keep in contact with constituents via email, letter and telephone.

Members of Parliament attend special events, such as the opening of a new community centre.

They meet with local councillors and Members of the Scottish Parliament (MSPs), and work with their local party.

Members of Parliament will sometimes give their backing to a local campaigns. They often use the media to raise their profile and that of any campaign which they are backing.

Activate your brain cells!

Think about where would be a good location and when would be a good time to hold a surgery in your local area. See if you can find out where your local MP's surgery takes place.

Work in parliament

The business hours of the UK Parliament run from Monday afternoon through to Friday afternoon. The parliament often runs late into the evening, although often the most important business is kept until the middle of the week to allow MPs to attend to any constituency business which they cannot see to over the weekends. MPs represent their constituents by participating in debates or by voting on **Bills**. MPs are able to put forward the topic for a debate as well as contribute to existing debates. They can also ask questions at Prime Minister's Question Time on issues which concern their constituents. MPs can put forward Private Members' Bills and participate in committees. Committees scrutinise Bills or the work of a particular government department, such as the Department of Health.

Bills: proposed laws

Pressures on Members of Parliament

Members of Parliament are constantly under a lot of pressure. Some MPs work in excess of 80 hours per week once their work in parliament, constituency work and travel time have been taken into account. Some

MPs have to travel from the very north of Scotland to London, and back, every week. Much of their constituency work must be done at weekends so that they can be in London on business days. MPs earn a generous basic salary of over £65,000 per year plus expenses, but must spend a lot of time away from their family. Many people think that MPs have a tougher job than MSPs because many have to travel so much further to get to parliament.

It is impossible for an MP to please all of his or her constituents. They also have to balance the wishes of their constituency with the wishes of their political party. If constituents think an MP is not representing them well in parliament, it is unlikely that they will vote for them in future elections.

Show your understanding

1. How often are MPs elected?
2. Copy the following table in your jotter. List the work that MPs do in their constituency and in parliament.

Constituency work	Parliamentary work

3. What pressures do MPs face?
4. What can constituents do if they think their MP is not representing them well?

Collect a skill

Support and oppose!

One key skill in Modern Studies is to be able to support and oppose a point of view.

Discuss with a partner whether or not you think MPs are paid too much for what they do. Make a list of arguments for and against the point of view.

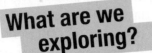
18 Why do we have a Scottish Parliament?

What are we exploring?

By the end of this section you should be able to:

▶ Explain why we have a Scottish Parliament
▶ Describe the difference between 'devolved' and 'reserved' powers

Scotland was an independent nation and had its own parliament until 1707, when the Act of Union was made between Scotland and England. Since that time, Scotland has been governed by the UK Parliament at Westminster.

In 1997, the Labour government at Westminster held a **referendum**, which asked the residents of Scotland whether or not they would like their own parliament. Almost 75% of voters were in favour of a Scottish Parliament. Voters were also in favour of the Scottish Parliament being permitted to raise or lower income tax by up to 3p per £1. This potentially means that the Scottish Government can either charge people less tax, or increase income tax to pay for government services. However, all governments in parliament so far have been reluctant to use this power.

> **referendum**: a vote in which the people in a country are asked to give their opinion or answer a question

The new Scottish Parliament came into being in 1999, using the Assembly Rooms of the Church of Scotland in Edinburgh as a base. It moved to a purpose-built building in 2004, just down the road at Holyrood. The Scottish Parliament building was very controversial, as the final cost of construction was 10 times more than first estimated, at an enormous £414.4 million. Many people feel that this was a significant waste of money.

The Scottish Parliament allows decisions to be made within Scotland on behalf of the Scottish people. Scotland's economy is much more reliant on industries such as tourism and fishing than the rest of the UK. Scotland also has lower life expectancy rates that most other Western European countries, and a poor health record. Having its own parliament has allowed Scotland to focus on these areas rather than being subject to decisions made at the UK Parliament, which may not always represent the best interest of the people of Scotland.

Although the Scottish Parliament can pass **legislation** specifically to meet the needs of Scottish people, it can only do this in some areas. These are called devolved powers. Scotland already had separate education and legal systems before the establishment of the new Scottish Parliament, so it made sense to continue with these as devolved powers. Most, however, are new powers for Scotland. The UK Parliament has kept control over some areas of society, and these are known as reserved powers.

> **legislation**: laws

? Bore your friends...

The concrete ceiling of each of the 129 MSPs' private offices is curved and weighs 18 tonnes!

Devolved powers – Scottish Parliament

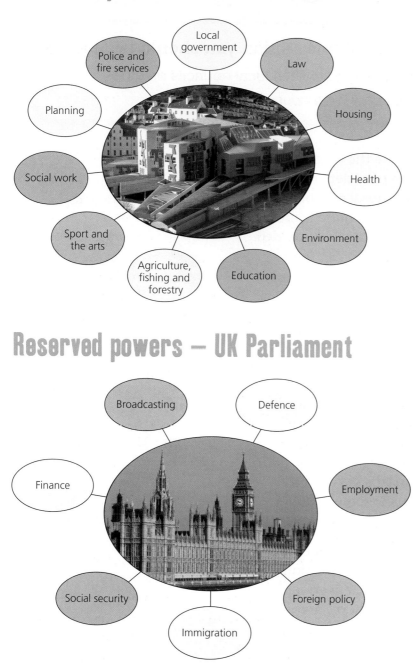

Local government

Police and fire services

Law

Planning

Housing

Social work

Health

Sport and the arts

Environment

Agriculture, fishing and forestry

Education

Reserved powers – UK Parliament

Broadcasting

Defence

Finance

Employment

Social security

Foreign policy

Immigration

Many of the reserved powers have been retained by the UK Parliament because it argues that they cover areas upon which it is very difficult to have a different laws in one part of the UK to another. Many people living in Scotland think that Scotland should have more power, and some think that Scotland would be better off if it was fully independent from the UK. This is what the current Scottish National Party (SNP) government of Scotland believes, and it is likely that it will have a referendum in the next few years to see if the Scottish population agrees with it.

Show your understanding

1. Why did the Labour government in 1997 decide to create a new Scottish Parliament?
2. Why do you think all of the governments in Scotland so far have been reluctant to use their tax-varying power?
3. Why do many people think the Scottish Parliament has benefited Scotland? Give examples to support your answer.
4. Do you think Scotland has enough powers? Give reasons for your answer.

19 What does my local government do?

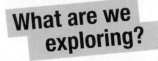

What are we exploring?

By the end of this section you should be able to:
▶ Describe what services local councils provide
▶ Explain how local councils are funded

In many ways, local government make the biggest contribution to the smooth running of society around us. Everyone within the UK lives in a local authority area, which you may know as your local council, and most of the day-to-day services that we use are provided by your local council.

In Scotland, there are 32 local councils. It would be far too difficult for the Scottish Parliament to focus on or understand the needs of each local community in Scotland. This is why this task is given over to the local councils. Local councils are required by law to provide many of the services in your area. These are called 'mandatory services'. The provisions of some services in your area are up to the local council itself, and usually depend on how much money a council has. These are called 'discretionary services'. During the recent recession in the UK, many local councils have reduced their provision of discretionary services to save money.

For example, education is a mandatory service and it is expected that all local councils in Scotland will ensure that all children of school age have a free education and the opportunity to sit a range of Scottish Qualifications Authority examinations in secondary school. Areas such as leisure facilities are discretionary, and whether they are provided or how much you must pay to use them will vary from council to council.

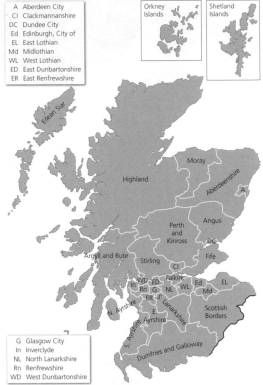

A Aberdeen City
Cl Clackmannanshire
DC Dundee City
Ed Edinburgh, City of
EL East Lothian
Md Midlothian
WL West Lothian
ED East Dunbartonshire
ER East Renfrewshire

Orkney Islands
Shetland Islands

Eilean Siar
Moray
Highland
Aberdeenshire
Perth and Kinross
Angus
DC
Argyll and Bute
Stirling
Cl
Fife
Falkirk
WD ED
In Rn G NL WL Ed EL
ER S Md
N. Ayrshire E. Lanarkshire
S. Ayrshire Ayrshire
Scottish Borders
Dumfries and Galloway

G Glasgow City
In Inverclyde
NL North Lanarkshire
Rn Renfrewshire
WD West Dunbartonshire

Table 19.1 Services provided by local government

Mandatory services (compulsory)	Discretionary services (optional)
Education (schools, teachers' salaries)	Leisure centre/sports facilities
Social work	Funding for youth programmes
Police and Fire Services	Adult education programmes (such as night classes)
Housing (council housing)	Theatres
Environmental services (e.g. waste collection, recycling facilities)	Funding services to support those with additional needs (e.g. BlindCraft, Edinburgh)
Roads (maintenance, public car parks)	

How are councils funded?

Local councils need money to pay for all of the services that they provide. The largest proportion of their funding (on average about 80%) comes directly from the Scottish Government as a **grant**. The remaining money is raised by the local councils themselves from council tax and non-domestic business rates. Local councils with large populations will be able to raise far more money themselves, and therefore receive a lower grant from the Scottish Government.

Council tax and non-domestic business rates are money which is directly paid to the local authority by each household or business to help pay for the services you use. How much council tax a household pays is based on the value of your house, regardless of whether you own it or rent it. Most local authorities raise additional money by charging people to use some of their services, such as leisure facilities or council house rent.

Activate your brain cells!

Can you think of any examples of how council cutbacks have affected your local area? Have any facilities closed down, or started charging more for their use? Write a list of any examples you can think of.

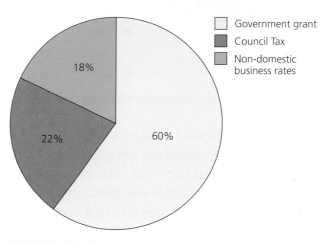

- ☐ Government grant
- ☐ Council Tax
- ☐ Non-domestic business rates

Edinburgh City Council Funding, 2010/2011.
Source: data from Edinburgh City Council

grant: a sum of money which is given and does not have to be repaid

Collect a skill

Exaggeration

Detecting exaggeration in Modern Studies is an important skill. Exaggeration means something is incorrect.

Finlay Brown said

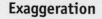

'The City of Edinburgh Council's sources of funding are close to the Scottish average'.

What evidence is there to suggest that Finlay Brown has exaggerated this comment?

Show your understanding

1. Why is local government often considered to be the most important level of government for British citizens?
2. Pick four services that local councils provide, which you use. Explain how you use these.
3. Explain how councils fund the services they provide.
4. Why do you think some people believe the council tax system is unfair?

Stretch yourself

Create a leaflet explaining the services that your local authority provides. You can usually find this information online or in your local library.

20 How do my local councillors represent me?

What are we exploring?

By the end of this section you should be able to:

▶ Describe how local councillors represent us

▶ Explain the difficulties councillors face when carrying out their work

▶ Write a letter to your local councillor

Local councillors are elected to represent the views of people when decisions are being made about how the council should be run. Local councils are broken up into several much smaller areas, called wards. Each ward usually has three or four councillors representing it, depending on its size. Wards usually only cover two or three villages, a town or part of a city. Councillors normally live within the area they represent and so have close contact with people living in the area and understand the needs and problems that the community faces.

Like Members of Parliament (MPs) and Members of the Scottish Parliament (MSPs), councillors hold regular surgeries in their local community to establish the needs or problems that exist within their area. They can also be contacted via telephone, email or letter. It is their responsibility to discuss problems brought to them by local people and vote on their behalf during meetings at the council chambers. Most councillors are members of a political party, so will usually share a similar ideology to that party.

Learning link

Look back at Chapter 11 to find out more about ideologies.

Activate your brain cells!

What problems in your local community would you like to discuss with your local councillor? Discuss with a partner.

Councillors have a responsibility to support local organisations, campaign on behalf of local issues and develop links with all parts of the community. Because they represent a much smaller area than MPs or MSPs, they have the opportunity to deal with more localised issues, such as campaigning for traffic-calming measures in a local village or campaigning against a primary school closure.

Local councillor at work

Slow down in our village

Caring about rural speeds

Many local councillors spend as much as 30 hours per week on council work. However, a councillor's basic salary in Scotland is approximately £16,000 plus expenses, which means many have to balance their council work with another job to ensure they earn enough money to have a good standard of living. Most people who become councillors do so because they want to serve their community, not because of the money. The Scottish Government is considering raising the basic salary of a councillor to reflect their enormous workload.

Protestors outside BlindCraft, Edinburgh

Councils across Scotland have faced huge cuts in recent years, as a consequence of the recession. This has made the work of councillors difficult in recent years, and they often have to make unpopular decisions.

The closure of the BlindCraft factory, Edinburgh

The BlindCraft factory has provided employment for the visually impaired in the Lothian region for over 200 years, making high-quality mattresses and bedding. This factory provided a lifeline for its employees, as many of them would find it very difficult to find fulfilling employment elsewhere. The factory ran at a loss, but because it provided vital support to 70 disabled employees, Edinburgh City Council subsidised the running costs by £1 million per year. In 2011, Edinburgh councillors voted in favour (40 to 18) of stopping subsidies to BlindCraft, forcing it to close. Like many local councils across Scotland, Edinburgh City Council is being forced to make savings of tens of millions of pounds over the next few years. It will be discretionary services that are worst affected by these cuts.

Stretch yourself

Write a letter to your local councillor describing some of the problems in your local community. Use Table 19.1 on page 38 to help you identify the areas that they are responsible for.

Show your understanding

1. List three things that councillors do to represent the people in their ward.
2. What challenges do councillors face when carrying out their work?
3. Do you think councillors earn enough money? Give reasons to support your answer.
4. Why did a majority of councillors in Edinburgh City Council vote to stop subsidising the BlindCraft factory?

21 What do trade unions do?

What are we exploring?

By the end of this section you should be able to:
▶ Explain what the purpose of a trade union is
▶ Describe what actions trade unions use to influence employers

In addition to the four levels of government that represent people in Scotland, there are also many organisations that represent the interests of individuals. One such organisation that many people are members of is a trade union, which aims to protect the rights of people at work.

What do trade unions do?

There are many different trade unions across the UK. Each individual trade union usually represent employees from particular industries, for example teachers, doctors or factory workers. The UK's largest union is UNITE (Union of Needletrades, Industrial and Textile Employees), which represents many manufacturing and transportation sector workers. It has over 2 million members nationwide. The main aims of all trade unions are:

- To ensure workers are paid fairly.
- To prevent major workplace changes, such as redundancy.
- To ensure safe working conditions for employees.
- To provide legal support for employees facing a disciplinary proceeding.
- To provide workers with benefits, such as discounted car insurance.

Trade unions are effective because employers are much more likely to listen to the opinions of a large number of workers than one individual worker. In most work places where trade unions are present, they

Union members forming a picket line during a strike

have a leader called a shop steward, who has been elected by members. The shop steward usually organises meetings with trade union members and negotiates with management on their behalf about their working conditions. When this is unsuccessful, members of trade unions use many other methods to make their voice heard. This is known as industrial action and includes:

- **Strikes:** stopping work for a period of time.
- **Overtime ban:** only working contracted hours.
- **Work to rule:** refusing to carry out any extra duties.

Activate your brain cells!

Think about why industrial action can be an effective. What impact can it have on an employer?

Trade union members also have many responsibilities. Trade union members have a responsibility to pay membership fees. These cover the running costs of the trade union and may be used to provide strike pay to members during industrial action. Although trade unions have a right to use industrial action, all members must have been formally balloted on whether or not they wish to participate in such action. If they agree, employers must be notified several weeks in advance of the industrial action taking place. Industrial action should be peaceful and trade union members must not break the law. If industrial action does not follow these procedures then trade union members would be breaking the law and may lose their jobs.

The use of industrial action by trade unions has become more common in the UK in recent years. This is because many industries have been affected by the recession, leading to companies trying to impose pay freezes, redundancies and changes in working conditions upon staff.

The airline British Airways (BA) tried to cut their staffing costs by reducing the number of crew on long-haul flights. Employees were outraged as it would make their job much more difficult, without extra pay. Many cabin crew employed by BA are members of the UNITE union. UNITE organised several strikes between March and May in 2010, grounding many flights and leading to huge losses for BA. As a result of the action, UNITE negotiated improved terms for staff.However, staff who participated in strikes were punished by BA by having their perks removed, such as free personal travel.

Collect a skill

Boost your word power!

Match up these heads and tails:

Strike action	Only working contracted hours
Redundancy	Stop working for a period of time
Shop steward	Action taken by trade union members
Overtime ban	Being dismissed from a job because they no longer need you
Industrial action	The leader of a trade union within a workplace

Show your understanding

1. Who do trade unions represent?
2. Which aim of trade unions do you think is most important? Give reasons for your answer.
3. How do shop stewards get their job?
4. List two responsibilities of trade union members?
5. Why did the UNITE union initiate industrial action on behalf of BA cabin crew?

22 What is the economy?

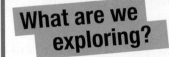

What are we exploring?

By the end of this section you should be able to:

▶ Explain what the economy is

▶ Describe how governments make money to run the services they provide

▶ Understand how capitalist economies work

The economy is the way in which countries make and use their money. Some countries, such as the UK, give individual citizens and businesses a lot of freedom to make money however they wish. This is what we call a **capitalist economy**. You can work for whoever you like, or even start your own business, without the government interfering. The opposite of capitalism is **communism.**

A capitalist government needs to make money to run the country. In order to make money, governments require individuals and businesses to pay a percentage of what they earn back to them in the form of taxes. This is called income tax. The money made from taxes is then used by the government to provide services such as schools, public transportation routes and healthcare. It also pays for the armed forces. All of the services which a government provides for its citizens are known as the public sector. The more money an individual or business makes, the more they will have to pay in taxes to the government. For this reason, the government is usually very happy to have successful businesses and individuals earning a high income in their country.

capitalist economy: an economy in which individuals are free to start up and grow businesses with very little interference from their country's government

communism: a system of government that tries to ensure that everyone is equal by keeping control over all aspects of the citizens' lives, such as business, jobs and housing

Learning link

To find out more about capitalism and communism, read Chapter 12.

 Activate your brain cells!

Most people do not like having to pay taxes. But what would our society be like if we did not pay tax? Can you think how things might change?

In a capitalist economy, companies must constantly compete with each other to remain successful. For example, a car manufacturer must constantly improve the design of its vehicles in order to keep persuading customers to buy them. If they do not do this, then customers may choose to buy another brand of car which they think has better fuel

Laptops have improved markedly over the years, partly due to competition

efficiency or more features, and the company would lose money and may go bankrupt. The competition between companies in a capitalist economy is good for customers. It means that the products we can choose from are constantly improving.

What is inflation?

Inflation is the name given to the general yearly increase in the price of goods and services. We cannot expect things to remain at the same price year after year. Inflation is measured as a percentage. For example, the average price of a packet of chewing gum 10 years ago was 26p. You can now expect to pay at least 50p for a packet of chewing gum in the UK. Our government tries to keep inflation low (around 2–3% per year), so that the cost of goods and services does not rise at a rate higher than people's salaries or wages. Most people expect a wage rise every year at approximately the same rate as inflation. This means that people should not be negatively affected by a rise in the cost of goods and services. However, not all products increase in price in line with inflation and some become cheaper to make and more widely available, for example laptops.

Competition is also good for customers because it helps to keep prices down. In addition to the quality of the product,

customers are also often concerned about how much it costs. This forces companies to constantly look at how they can reduce the costs of making a particular item. If they did not do this, then customers may choose to buy a product, such as a car, from another company which sells vehicles of the same quality but at a lower price.

A good example of how this has benefited customers is the laptop computer. Laptops are now 90% cheaper on average than they were in 2000, because laptop manufacturers have constantly improved their technology and found ways of making them much more cheaply. Competition is an essential part of business. Companies that do not have any competition have no incentive to improve or reduce the price of their product. This is called a monopoly.

Show your understanding

1. What is the 'economy'?
2. What is a capitalist economy?
3. What is a communist political system?
4. How do governments make money?
5. Why do governments want businesses in their country to be successful?
6. Explain two reasons why competition between companies is good for customers.
7. What is a monopoly?

23 What is a multinational company?

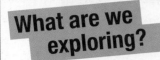

By the end of this section you should be able to:

▶ Understand what a multinational company is
▶ Describe the advantages and disadvantages of multinational companies setting up factories in developing countries

Trade is very important for a country's economy. Trade is the buying and selling of a product. How wealthy a country is depends on how successful the businesses and industries are within it. Many companies now trade or have branches in more than one country. These are known as multinational companies, or MNCs. Usually, the MNC will have its headquarters in its home country but will manufacture its product and trade all over the world.

Multinational companies have existed for centuries. One of the oldest MNCs is the Hudson Bay Company, which started in the seventeenth century. The Hudson Bay Company began importing goods that it obtained in North America, such as furs, to sell in the European market. It bought these goods from the Cree people, who lived in northern Canada, and sold them at a profit to customers across Europe. The Hudson Bay Company still exists today and mainly makes and sells clothing. It is most famous for providing clothing for the Canadian winter and summer Olympic teams.

One of the most famous MNCs is McDonald's. Two brothers started McDonald's in 1940 in California, with only one restaurant. They invented the 'Speedee Service System', which later became known as 'fast food'. Over the last 70 years, McDonald's has expanded to over 119 countries and employs 1.5 million people across the world. Over 58 million customers are served across the world each day in McDonald's restaurants, and it is very common to see or visit the famous golden arches when travelling abroad.

The Hudson's Bay Company still provides clothing for the Canadian Olympic team

There are McDonald's restaurants in 119 countries around the world

Activate your brain cells!

What other multinational companies can you think of? Create a list with a partner.

Are multinational companies a good or a bad thing?

Multinational companies can have both a positive and negative impact on the countries they conduct their business in. When MNCs expand, they often choose to open factories in developing countries to make their product. This can benefit developing countries as it provides jobs and can boost their economy. This can help citizens in these countries to become better-off and can provide the much needed money that a country needs to improve services, such as transportation and communications.

However, there is also a downside to this. One of the reasons that MNCs often choose to make or source their product in a developing country is because people expect to work far longer hours for much less money. MNCs also are also attracted to the fact that many developing countries demand much lower health and safety standards in the workplace than a developed country. Both factors make it much cheaper for MNCs to locate there. As a consequence, many employees in factories in developing countries which are owned by MNCs work in terrible conditions with few breaks and earn very little. Factories where these conditions occur are often referred to as 'sweatshops'. It is usually the developed country where a particular MNC is based that profits most, as most of the products made and profits are returned there. Others would argue that MNCs at least are providing jobs in areas where previously there has often been high unemployment.

It is not uncommon for goods that we use, particularly clothes and sports equipment, to made by child labour. It is estimated that in Pakistan alone there are around 10 million children labourers under the age of 14 years. The BBC did an undercover report in 1996, which exposed the fact that many of the leading sports brands were selling footballs stitched together by children in Pakistan. Most of these children were earning little more than 20p per day and working for up to 12 hours each day. As a result of this report, most leading football brands have now committed to ensuring that their footballs are not made by children.

Show your understanding

1. What is a multinational company?
2. Write a list of five multinational companies that you can think of.
3. How can multinational companies benefit a developing country?
4. How can a multinational company sometimes be bad for a developing country?
5. What methods do you think you could use to ensure that you are not buying products made either in a 'sweatshop' or by child labour.

REVIEW

Create a poster to convince people not to buy products from companies that use sweatshops to produce their goods.

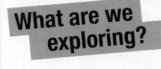

What is a recession?

> **What are we exploring?**
>
> **By the end of this section you should be able to:**
> ▶ Understand the causes of the most recent recession
> ▶ Create a flow diagram to simplify an idea

When trade is slow, it can mean that individuals will make less money and businesses make less profit. This can mean that businesses find it difficult to pay staff and can lead to people being made redundant. When this problem affects an entire country, it is known as a recession.

Most countries trade heavily with other foreign countries and rely on this to make money. This is known as **interdependence**. When one country, such as the USA, is experiencing a recession, it often triggers a recession in the countries it trades with as well, such as the UK. This is because the UK is reliant on foreign countries buying its products to make money. In other words, when other countries stop buying our products, because they have less money, it means that the UK is also unable to make money.

> interdependence: when countries are reliant on buying and selling goods to each other to make money

What caused the most recent global recession?

The combination of interdependency and a reduction in the amount of trading between countries has led to a global recession. This current recession, which began in 2008, started because the value of people's houses had gone down.

How can falling house prices cause a recession?

When they buy a house, most people cannot usually afford to pay the full amount that it is sold for. Instead, they usually pay a small deposit and borrow the rest of the money from a bank in the form of a loan, called a mortgage. Mortgages are paid off over a very long time, sometimes as much as 25 or 30 years. Many people sell their homes before they have paid off their mortgage completely. Homes usually go up in value over time (unlike goods such as cars and computers), so this normally allows people to sell their home at a profit, pay off the remainder of their mortgage and be left with some money to put towards a bigger house.

Because the banks that provide the mortgages assumed that house prices would continue to rise, they lent many buyers

Falling house values started the recession in 2008

more money than the house was worth, thinking that over time the value of the houses would go up and borrowers would be able to repay the higher loan when they sold the house. In the end, house prices fell in many countries, such as the USA and the UK. This meant that many people discovered that they had borrowed far more money than their house was worth, and even if they sold the property they would not be able to pay back all of the loan.

Banks suddenly realised that they had lost huge sums of money through this process of lending people too much money. Some banks went bankrupt, causing individuals, businesses and even governments to lose huge sums of money they had saved with these banks. In the UK, the government loaned several banks money to prevent them from going bankrupt. This left the government with less to spend on providing services for British citizens. People started to spend less because they were worried that they might run out of money or be made unemployed. This meant in turn that shops and businesses were losing money too, as they were not selling as many goods and services. Many of their employees were made redundant because their employers could no longer afford to pay them. This leads to people having even less money to spend.

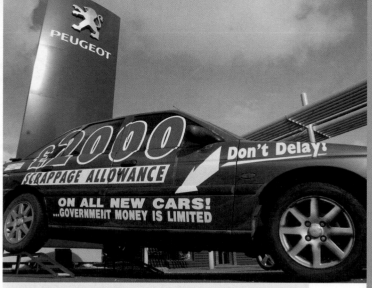

Car salesroom advertising the scrappage scheme

How has the UK government tried to end the recession?

The UK government has put many measures in place to try to bring an end to the recession. One thing that it has tried to do is encourage people to spend money again, as this boosts shops and businesses. It temporarily reduced VAT (value-added tax: the tax we pay on bought goods) to make general shopping cheaper. The government also financed initiatives such as the car scrappage scheme, which encouraged people to buy a brand-new car by giving them £2000 towards it. This was aimed at helping the car industry in the UK, which employs thousands of people. Despite all of these initiatives, it is still unclear when the current recession will end.

Collect a skill

Create a diagram

Diagrams can help us simplify difficult ideas.

Using the information from this chapter, display the process that led to the current recession as flow diagram. It has been started for you:

> House values fell → Banks had loaned people more money than their houses were worth

Show your understanding

1. What is a recession?
2. Why did falling house prices cause the current recession to begin?
3. How can people not buying goods and services lead to unemployment?
4. Give examples of two measures that the UK government has put in place to try to end the current recession.

25 How does the UK government help the unemployed?

What are we exploring?

By the end of this section you should be able to:

▶ Identify how the UK government measures the number of unemployed people in the UK

▶ Describe how the government provides financial support to the unemployed

▶ Describe how the government helps the unemployed to find new jobs

Many people in the UK have become unemployed since the beginning of the recession in 2008. 7.8% of the UK working population is currently unemployed. This has risen by over 2% since the beginning of the recession in 2008. The government only classes people as officially unemployed if they meet the following criteria:

- They do not have a job of any kind.
- They are actively looking for work.
- They are receiving Jobseeker's Allowance.

The government is keen to support as many people as possible back into work, as it costs a lot of money to support the unemployed, leaving the government with less money to spend on other services.

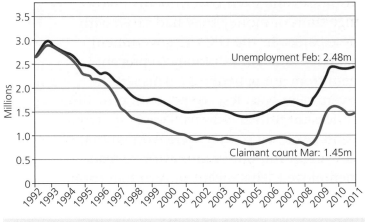

Unemployment Feb: 2.48m

Claimant count Mar: 1.45m

Unemployment in the UK, 1992–2001. Source: data from Office for National Statistics

Activate your brain cells!

Think about it! Why do you think the government only includes people who meet the criteria opposite in its official statistics of the number of unemployed?

How does the government provide financial support to the unemployed?

One of the main problems that people who become unemployed face is paying for essentials such as housing, food and heating costs and supporting their family.

One of the main benefits which the government provides for the unemployed is Jobseeker's Allowance. This is a small amount of money which you are paid every 2 weeks to help you make ends meet until you find a new job. You must be between the ages of 18 and 65 years to receive this and how much you receive is based on how much National Insurance you paid while you were working. The most that a person over the age of 25 years can receive is £65.55 per week. If you are between 18 and 24 years old, you will only receive a maximum of £51.85 per week

National Insurance is taken off your wages before you receive them, in addition to income tax. It goes towards paying for healthcare, pensions and Jobseeker's Allowance for British citizens. You must have paid this for at least 2 years before becoming unemployed to receive the maximum Jobseeker's Allowance payment. To continue receiving the benefit, you must attend a meeting with a representative from the Jobcentre every 2 weeks with evidence that proves you have been looking for a job.

In addition to this, unemployed people who are receiving Jobseeker's Allowance may be entitled to receive other benefits to help pay their general living expenses. These include housing benefit to help them pay their rent and council tax benefit to help them pay the charge that all householders pay towards the cost of local services, e.g. schools, bin collection, street lighting.

How does the government help the unemployed to find new jobs?

The UK government has set up the Jobcentre to help people find new employment. Unemployed people can go here to find out about job vacancies and get help filling in application forms. The Jobcentre also provides support to help people prepare for job interviews and get

any training they might require to help them find a job, such as IT (information technology) skills.

The UK government has set up a 'new deal' scheme to support unemployed people back into work. As well as providing support with job applications and interviews, this also helps to find suitable work experience, volunteering opportunities or further education for unemployed individuals in order to increase their skills and hopefully find a new job more easily. It is usually compulsory for unemployed people to participate in the new deal scheme if they have not successfully found new employment after 3 months. If they do not participate, they will stop receiving Jobseeker's Allowance.

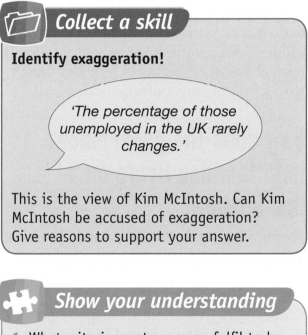

📁 Collect a skill

Identify exaggeration!

'The percentage of those unemployed in the UK rarely changes.'

This is the view of Kim McIntosh. Can Kim McIntosh be accused of exaggeration? Give reasons to support your answer.

🧩 Show your understanding

1. What criteria must a person fulfil to be classified by the government as unemployed?
2. For what other reasons might a person not have a job, other than redundancy?
3. Give two examples of ways in which the government provides financial support to the unemployed.
4. Give two examples of ways in which the government provides unemployed people with support in finding a new job.

How does the government help other people with needs?

What are we exploring?

By the end of this section you should be able to:

▶ Understand the difference between financial and social support

▶ Explain how the government helps those on a low income, the disabled and the elderly

There are many other people who need extra help to make ends meet or find employment. The UK government provides several financial benefits and social support schemes to help those living on a low income. It also helps parents with children, the disabled and the elderly. A financial benefit is one that helps a person with money. Social support is one which helps protect a person's rights or provides them with physical and emotional care.

How does the government help families living on a low income?

People who live on a low income can find it difficult to make ends meet. They might be living on a low income because they earn a low salary or work part-time. Many people who earn a low income are also eligible to receive housing benefit and council tax benefit.

Since 1999, the UK government has enforced a national minimum wage in order to make sure people earn a decent living. This is the minimum hourly rate which employers must pay their staff who are aged 21 years or over. People on a low income may also receive working tax credit, or child tax credit if they have a family. These both allow you to pay a little less income tax so

that you have more money to spend on the essentials you need for daily living. Tax credits encourage people to work full-time by making sure that they will be better-off when working to earn money, rather than relying on benefits.

How does the government support disabled people?

The government supports disabled people by helping them to meet their financial needs through Disability Allowance. This helps disabled people to cover any extra costs that they may face because of their disability. It can help individuals to pay for any care that they need, or any equipment that they need if they have mobility issues.

Some disabled people are eligible for the Motability Scheme as part of their Disability Allowance. This provides financial help for disabled people to buy a car. Through this scheme, cars are adapted to meet the physical requirements of the customer, and are insured and regularly serviced to ensure they do not break down. This scheme provides a lifeline to many disabled people who would otherwise find it very difficult to get around or drive a standard vehicle. The government has also made a law, called the Disability and Equality Act 2010, to protect the rights of disabled people. This law is important because it requires almost all areas of society, such as public transport, schools and employers, to make provisions to allow disabled people to access their services or work.

How does the government support the elderly?

Most men aged over 65 years and women aged over 60 years receive a state pension from the government. Many elderly people can find it very difficult to make ends meet when they retire and no longer have a regular wage or salary coming in. Most people prepare for their retirement throughout their working life by paying a pension through their workplace, called an occupational pension, and through saving. However, even with this, many retired people find that they have a lot less, money each month than when they were working and still worry about paying for basics such as bills. The government also gives people who are over the age of 60 years a one-off winter fuel payment every year, which can be up to £300. This will help an elderly person to pay for the higher heating costs which are associated with the cold winter period.

Motability scheme vehicle

The elderly receive a state pension to help them make ends meet

Show your understanding

1. What is a financial support?
2. What is meant by social support?
3. What is working tax credit and child tax credit?
4. What special needs might a disabled person have when driving a car, and how does the Motability Scheme help them meet these needs?
5. What financial problems might an elderly person face?
6. How does the government provide financial support for the elderly?

Explore further

Do you know how much things cost?
How much money do you think a family of four will need each week to cover its basic needs? With a partner, identify what your basic needs are and how much it would cost a family of four (two parents and two children) to cover these for a week. Compare your notes with other members of the class. Are there any things that you have that you would you consider to be non-essential, or luxuries?

Stretch yourself

Research what rights are protected for disabled people under the Disability and Equality Act 2010.

27 Why study the USA?

What are we exploring?

By the end of this chapter you should be able to:

▶ Explain why the USA is an important country

▶ Explain why we the UK has strong links with the USA

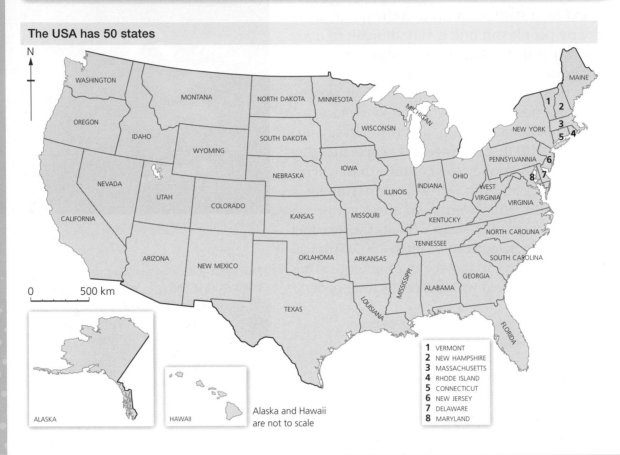

The USA has 50 states

1 VERMONT
2 NEW HAMPSHIRE
3 MASSACHUSETTS
4 RHODE ISLAND
5 CONNECTICUT
6 NEW JERSEY
7 DELAWARE
8 MARYLAND

Alaska and Hawaii are not to scale

The USA is one of the most important countries in the world. It is a relatively new country by world standards, and has only existed in its current form since the Declaration of Independence in 1776. However, it was **colonised** by Europeans in 1492 and groups of Native Americans have lived in the areas that are now part of the USA since long before that. The USA has a long history of different nationalities and ethnic groups battling over land and rights. One of the most turbulent points in recent US history was the battle between the northern and southern states during the Civil War. The dispute was over the enslavement of Africans in the southern

The USA is the third largest country in the world. It covers a slightly larger land area than China, but has a much smaller population.

It is separated into 50 states – 48 are on the mainland, but Alaska and Hawaii are not.

It has a population of 312 million people.

The USA has one of the five permanent seats on the United Nations (UN) security council.

It is the richest country in the world.

states, which the northern states disapproved of. It led to a bloody civil war between 1861 and 1865, resulting in the death of nearly 700,000 soldiers. This is more than the number of American troops that have been killed in all conflicts that they have been involved in since, including World War One, World War Two and the Vietnam War. Even after the abolishment of slavery in 1865, the USA continues to this day to have a number of disputes and problems regarding the rights of the various ethnic groups who live within the country.

colonised: when a large number of citizens from one country move to another and set up a permanent settlement

The USA has a large influence on our culture from the products we use and what we eat and do through to the music we listen to. The USA has become one of the richest countries in the world because of its strong industrial sector. It is one of the main exporters of hi-tech electrical goods, cars and military technology. Many multinational companies are based in the USA, and we use products and services that originate from the USA every day. US companies such as Microsoft and McDonald's can be found in almost every country in the world and have made their founders very rich. Even most of the movies and a large proportion of the television shows we watch are set and produced in the USA. Not only do we rely on US companies for many of the goods and services we use, but they also provide us with a huge market to trade with.

Learning link

To find out more about multinational companies, look at Chapter 23.

Activate your brain cells!

How does the USA influence your life? Discuss with a partner.

The USA is also an important **ally** to the UK. It has the second largest military in the world (after China) but is widely regarded to be the most powerful because of the hugely sophisticated military technology that it has. The UK's military is much smaller and often we have relied on the USA to support us with their armed forces in most of the conflicts that we have been involved in.

ally: a country or person with whom you work to reach a common goal

Show your understanding

1. Why would we describe the USA as a relatively new country?
2. Why did the Civil War break out?
3. Why has the USA become one of the richest countries in the world?
4. Name four multinational companies that you can think of that originate in the USA.
5. Make a spider diagram listing all of the ways in which the USA influences your life (you may want to consider products you use, the media, etc.).

Collect a skill

Support with evidence

'The USA is an important ally to the UK'.

This is the view of the UK government spokesperson. Do you agree with this view? Provide evidence to support your answer.

Stretch yourself

Find out how many stars and stripes the US flag has and why.

Bore your friends…

The entire land area of the UK could fit 2.84 times into the state of Texas.

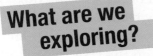

How is the USA governed?

What are we exploring?

By the end of this chapter you should be able to:
▶ Explain what the US constitution is
▶ Describe how laws are made by the US government

The US Constitution protects the rights of US citizens. The Constitution is a set of rules that outline how the country should be run. It states what powers the government should have and what rights US citizens should have. The Bill of Rights is the part of the US Constitution that focuses on what rights citizens should have. If US citizens think they are being denied the right to do something that is protected by the Bill of Rights, they can go to court.

The Bill of Rights is made up of 10 rules. Here are some of them.

+ *enjoy freedom of press, the right to protest and to practise whatever religion they wish*
+ *own a gun*
+ *have a fair trial*
+ *not be tortured, even if they have committed a crime*
+ *not have their rights denied by others.*

Any new laws that are made by the US government must be compatible with the US Constitution, otherwise they will be thrown out. The Constitution is regarded as one of the most important pieces of legislation ever made in the USA, and citizens take their Constitution very seriously. Some citizens argue that there are laws, such as the right to own a gun, which are no longer necessary in modern times and should be removed. However, it is very difficult to change the Constitution. This has meant that most rules within it have remained the same for over 200 years. There is no constitution in the UK, which makes it much easier to change laws in this country.

Activate your brain cells!

Think about the US Bill of Rights. Are there any that you would add or change? Discuss with a partner and give reasons for your changes.

The USA has a slightly different style of government to that which we are used to in the UK. In the UK, laws are made by the UK Parliament. In Scotland, many of the laws are made by the Scottish Parliament. In both parliaments, laws must be signed by the monarch (the Queen) before they can have fully become a law. In the USA, they have no monarchy so they have a presidential style of government instead. The powers of the US government are separated between three branches. This is to stop any one branch becoming too powerful. A Bill must be passed by all three branches to become a law.

Here are the three branches of the US government:

1. Congress: This is made up of the House of Representatives and the Senate. They take forward the ideas of US citizens and vote on Bills. If a Bill receives a majority vote in both houses, it is then passed to the president for his approval.

2. President: The president must sign a Bill after it has passed through Congress for it to become law.

3. Supreme Court: The Supreme Court makes sure that the law is followed and that all new laws comply with the US Constitution.

Congress   President Obama   The Supreme Court

Show your understanding

1. What is the purpose of the US Constitution?
2. How does the Constitution affect laws made in the USA?
3. Explain one difference between the system of government in the USA and that in the UK.
4. Why are there three branches of government in the USA?
5. Describe how a law is passed in the USA.

Collect a skill

Support and oppose!

List the arguments for and against people being allowed to own a gun. What do you think? Give reasons for your answer.

Stretch yourself

Create a Bill of Rights for Scotland.

Make a poster listing the rights that you think should be protected for people in Scotland.

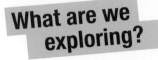
29 How powerful is the US president?

What are we exploring?

By the end of this chapter you should be able to:
- ▶ Describe the powers of the US president
- ▶ Explain the limitations upon the powers of the president

There have been 44 different US presidents since the USA officially formed. The US president is the leader of one of the richest countries in the world, with one of the most powerful armies in the world. For this reason, many people regard the US president as the most powerful individual in the world.

Commander in Chief of the US army

Although the US army is not the largest in the world, it is probably the most technologically advanced. This makes it a very powerful enemy to any state that is in conflict with it, and a very powerful ally to any country that works alongside it (such as the UK). The US president is the official leader of the army and he can decide where and when US armed forces are deployed. For example, in 2009 President Obama decided that a further 30,000 troops should be sent to Afghanistan. However, the president must get approval from Congress when he declares war.

Why is the US president so powerful?

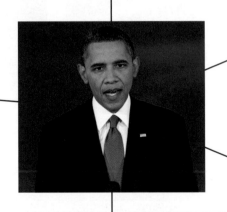

Power to make legislation

Although there are three branches of government which most new laws must pass through in order to stop one branch becoming too powerful, the US president does actually have the power to make laws without them being approved by Congress. These are known as 'Executive Orders'. However, this power is often only used in an emergency, when laws need to be made quickly. For example, former President George Bush, Jr, made an executive order straight after the September 11 attacks to create the Office of Homeland Security in order to make it more difficult for potential terrorists to travel the USA.

? Bore your friends...

The average age of US presidents when they take office is 55 years old.

Chief Ambassador for the USA

The USA has many foreign embassies in countries around the world. These represent the interests of the USA and US citizens in the countries where they are located. Each embassy is managed by a

President Obama with other foreign leaders

US ambassador. Each ambassador is chosen by the US president and is appointed for a period of 4 years. Ambassadors are chosen very carefully to ensure that the USA enjoys a positive relationship with the country that their embassy is within. However, the US president is the main ambassador to all countries and often meets with foreign leaders from other countries to negotiate trade agreements or resolve conflicts.

veto power: stop a Bill being passed
undemocratic: making decisions without taking into account the views of citizens

Power to veto legislation

The US president also has the power to veto legislation. Once a Bill has passed through Congress, it must be signed by the president to become a law. It he does not agree with the law, the president may use his veto power. Bush used his **veto power** in 2006 to stop a Bill permitting stem cell research using aborted foetuses. The Republican Party, to which he belonged, is generally anti-abortion and therefore it was seen as acceptable that he used his veto power here. However, as with 'Executive Orders', most presidents do not overuse this power as it is viewed as being **undemocratic.**

Show your understanding

1. Why do many people regard the US president as the most powerful individual in the world?
2. What power does the US president have over the US armed forces?
3. What influence does Congress have over the armed forces?
4. What is an 'Executive Order'?
5. When are Executive Orders often used?
6. Explain why presidents try not to overuse Executive Orders or their veto power.

30 Who are the Americans?

What are we exploring?

By the end of this chapter you should be able to:

▶ Identify the different ethnic groups that make up the US population

▶ Explain why these groups have settled in the USA

▶ Be able to make conclusions based upon evidence given

The USA was colonised by many different countries from around the world, and most US citizens today can trace their families history back to another country in two or three generations. This has created a very diverse culture in the USA, which sometimes is referred to as a 'melting pot'. The only descendants of the original inhabitants of the USA are Native Americans, who account for only 1% of the US population. The largest ethnic group in the USA are whites (65%), most of whom are descendants of the original European colonists. All other groups in the USA are known as ethnic minorities.

Table 30.1 Ethnic groups: percentage of total population in 2011 (total population – 312,000,000)

Ethnic group	% of total population
White	65
Hispanic	16
African American (black)	13
Asian and Pacific Islanders	5
Native Americans	1
Total population	100

Table 30.2 Ethnic groups: percentage of total population – estimated for the year 2050 (estimated total population – 420,000,000)

Ethnic group	% of total population
White	47
Hispanic	29
African American (black)	14
Asian and Pacific Islanders	9
Native Americans	1
Total population	100

Ethnic minorities in the USA

Hispanics

Hispanics are the largest ethnic minority in the USA

Hispanics are the fastest growing ethnic minority group in the USA. They originate from Mexico, Puerto Rico and Cuba and speak Spanish as their first language. Mexican and Puerto Rican Hispanics have mainly come in search of the 'American Dream' and are economic migrants. Most Cubans have come to escape the communist regime in Cuba, and are both political and economic migrants. A large number of Hispanics come to the USA illegally in order to seek a better life.

Activate your brain cells!

Think about it. What big changes could a larger Hispanic population make to US culture?

Native Americans

Native Americans are the only truly original inhabitants of the USA. They were forced off much of the land they occupied in North America by European colonists into areas known as reservations, where many of them remain today. There are still many legal disputes taking place in the USA between Native Americans and others groups over rightful land ownership.

Oprah Winfrey is a famous African American

A Native American

African Americans

Most African Americans are descended from African slaves brought over to work in plantations in the southern states of the USA. African Americans dispersed all across the USA after slavery was abolished, and there are large concentrations within inner-city areas of most major US cities.

Asian and Pacific Islanders

Asian and Pacific Islanders (APIs) originate from countries in Asia and the Pacific region, including Japan, China and South Korea. Many APIs are now second or third generation.

Show your understanding

1. Why is the US population sometimes referred to as a 'melting pot'?
2. What is the largest ethnic group in the USA?
3. In what ways do you think the enormous growth of the Hispanic population might affect US culture?
4. Who are African Americans descended from?
5. Who can be described as the original Americans?
6. What problems did colonisation cause for the original Americans?

Collect a skill

Being able to make conclusions from evidence you are given is an important skill for life. A conclusion is a statement about a particular issue, based on facts. Using Tables 30.1 and 30.2, you should be able to make conclusions about the following. Back your conclusions up with evidence from the table.

What is the expected level of population change between 2011 and 2050 for whites, Hispanics, African Americans?

31 Is everyone in the USA equal?

What are we exploring?

By the end of this chapter you should be able to:

▶ Explain what is mean by the American Dream
▶ Describe the inequalities that many groups in the USA face
▶ Explain the reasons for these inequalities

Most ethnic groups originally moved to the USA in search of the **American Dream**. This is the belief that the USA is the land of opportunity, and if you work hard, you will become successful and wealthy. The American Dream has not, however, been a reality for everyone, and there are many examples of areas in US society where huge **inequalities** exist. There are many reasons for these inequalities and it is often ethnic minorities who are worst affected.

American Dream: the belief that, in the USA, everyone has the opportunity to achieve a good standard of living as long as they are prepared to work hard
inequalities: people are not all equal

Jobs and income

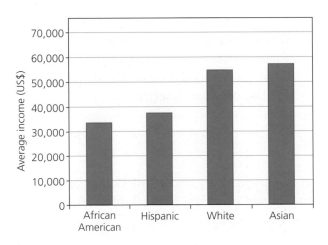

There is a huge gap between the richest and poorest people within the USA. The average income of the various ethnic groups in the USA varies enormously. The poorest group in the USA is African Americans, closely followed by Hispanics. The reasons for African American and Hispanic poverty can be partially linked to the poorer level of education that both groups tend to have.

Both groups experience higher educational dropout rates than whites. In 2008, 9.9% of African American and 18.4% of Hispanic students left high school without qualifications, compared with 4.0% of whites. This means both groups are less likely to get well-paid jobs. However, African Americans are more likely to be unemployed and rely on welfare, which causes their poverty, whereas Hispanics are much more likely to work, just in a low-paid job. Asians, on the other hand, have extremely low dropout rates and are most likely to go on to university.

Health

Table 31.1 Life expectancy in the USA

Ethnic group	White	African American	Hispanic	Asian
Life expectancy (years)	78	70	80	84

The USA is very different to the UK in the way it provides healthcare, as individuals must pay for it themselves. As it is very expensive, most Americans pay for their healthcare with health insurance. Americans who have well-paid jobs often have this provided for them by their employer, as insurance alone costs several thousand dollars per year. Those who have health insurance have access to some of the best healthcare in the world. Those who do not are lucky if they can get anything beyond emergency care.

African Americans and Hispanics tend to have the lowest levels of healthcare, and often therefore cannot access the treatment they need. However, despite this, Hispanics have a reasonably high life expectancy because they tend to live slightly healthier lifestyles than African Americans. However, many Hispanics still struggle to pay for healthcare if they experience any major illnesses.

An African American male is eight times more likely to go to prison than a white male

The availability of guns in the USA has made the nature of much of the violence much more serious. A third of all African American males will end up in prison, disabled or dead by the time they are 30 years old.

Hispanics also become involved in crime as a result of poverty, but not to the same extent as African Americans. Many believe the reason for this is that Hispanics often have strong family values, which tend to keep them out of trouble.

Activate your brain cells!

Think about what factors might cause whites to have a lower life expectancy than Hispanics, despite being more likely to have health insurance. Why do you think African American life expectancy is even lower?

Crime

African Americans are more likely to commit and be the victims of crime than any other ethnic group. The reasons for this are very much linked to poverty. Many African Americans are born to single-parent families with little or no income living in ghetto areas of cities. With little prospects, huge numbers turn to life in gangs to provide them with a sense of family and safety. Many turn to taking drugs, or sometimes even sell drugs to make money.

Show your understanding

1. What is the American Dream?
2. Using Table 31.1, give evidence to show that there are inequalities in wealth between different ethnic groups.
3. Explain why African Americans and Hispanics have lower average incomes.
4. Create a bar graph showing differences in life expectancy, based on Table 32.2. You can use the lines in your jotter to help you.
5. Why do African Americans and Hispanics suffer inequalities in health?
6. Which group is most likely to become involved in crime, and why? Give evidence to support your answer.
7. Which ethnic minority does appear to have achieved the American Dream? Provide evidence to support your answer.

32 Are things getting better for ethnic minorities in the USA?

What are we exploring?

By the end of this chapter you should be able to:

▶ Describe examples of progress for ethnic minorities
▶ Identify examples of ethnic minority success, using examples
▶ Explain why Asians have been so successful in the USA

There is evidence that things are improving for ethnic minorities. The number of African Americans and Hispanics living in poverty has gone down, which is partly the result of lower school dropout rates and hence better qualifications, better jobs and a higher income. However, the gap between those who are richest and those who are poorest is rising.

Recent governments have tried to tackle some of the inequalities that particular groups within society face. President Obama has tried to improve access to healthcare for all by implementing healthcare reforms, which should extend cover to an extra 32 million people in the USA. This would particularly help children in low-income families, who are often the worst affected by their parents' inability to pay for adequate healthcare. However, many in Congress are against this policy, meaning that future governments could overturn it.

Activate your brain cells!

Why do you think that many Americans are against healthcare reform? Discuss with a partner.

Ethnic minorities and the American Dream

Some individuals do manage to achieve the American Dream. There are now many high-profile African Americans and Hispanics who have managed to become very successful. Barack Obama is the first African American president. Hispanic singer and actress, Jennifer Lopez, has become very successful despite coming from a very modest family in the Bronx. She financed her early singing career through working in a legal office and from dancing in a Manhattan nightclub. She became noticed after dancing on several rap videos in the early 1990s, and eventually became very successful in her own right, producing several albums. These stories are, however, still the exception to the norm for many African American and Hispanic citizens.

Asians, however, have been incredibly successful in the USA – more successful than whites in many cases. They have the highest average income, the highest level of college graduates, and the longest life expectancy and many run successful businesses or are employed in well-paid jobs in the fields of science and engineering.

Why have Asians been so successful in the USA?

Asians are often thought to be so successful because of their cultural values. They tend to have strong family units that keep them away from trouble such as crime and drugs. They also have very low levels of teenage pregnancy. As a group, Asians have always valued education highly as a way to become successful. Most Asian families place a lot of emphasis on their children achieving good qualifications at school level and beyond. Many have excelled in the fields of science and engineering, which are often the most well-paid jobs in the USA. They have excellent health because most still adhere to a typically Asian diet, which tends to be less fatty than the diet of the average white American.

On the other hand, Asians are increasingly becoming the victims of hate crimes. It is believed this is because in many parts of the USA, particularly areas such as California, there is an increasing anti-immigrant feeling. Many Asian business owners are finding their premises vandalised or burgled, and the number of physical and verbal attacks upon Asians has increased by 17% over that last 5 years. Even for this very successful group, achieving the American Dream is not straightforward.

Asian Americans have been particularly successful in science and engineering

⊞ Show your understanding

1. What evidence is there that ethnic minorities are facing fewer inequalities than in the past?
2. How had President Obama tried to reduce inequalities in health? What problems may he face in the future?
3. Describe how Jennifer Lopez achieved the American Dream.
4. Give three reasons why Asians have been so successful in the USA.
5. What problems do Asians still face as a group?

🔍 Explore further

Find out a bit more about the life of a famous US ethnic minority citizen who has achieved the American Dream. Use the Internet to find out about the person you have chosen, and write a short biography explaining how he or she became successful. Try to use more than one source of information, and record your sources carefully.

33 What is an international alliance?

What are we exploring?

By the end of this section you should be able to:

▶ Explain why international alliances exist

▶ Describe the different types of international alliances

An international alliance is when a group of countries join together to make themselves richer and safer. There are a number of different international alliances across the world, all with different purposes. Countries choose to join international alliances for two main reasons. These are:

- economic: to make all member countries richer
- security: to protect member countries from attack and protect their interests (such as oil reserves).

Most international alliances exist for either economic or security reasons, and many exist for both reasons.

David Cameron negotiated new trade agreeme with China in 2010

Economic alliances try to protect the financial interests of their member countries and make them wealthier. They do this by negotiating agreements to make it easier to **trade** or set up companies in other member states. There are many examples of groups of countries that have done this and these arrangements are often known as **free trade agreements**. In 2010, new agreements were made between the UK and Chinese governments to make trading less restrictive between the two countries. This made it possible for a British company, Rolls Royce, to secure a deal worth £740 million to supply and maintain engines for a Chinese airline. This is good for both countries.

trade: buying and selling goods

free trade agreement: allowing other countries to buy and sell goods in your country with no or reduced export and import tax

Security alliances are designed to prevent attacks and to protect the property and rights of member countries. The North Atlantic Treaty Organization (NATO) is an example of a security alliance made up of the USA and several European nations. All of the member countries of NATO combined create a massive and technologically advanced military resource that has the potential force to deal with most types of attack. An attack made upon one member country is viewed as 'an attack on all', and all member countries would be expected to provide military support if an event such as this happens.

Countries also form security alliances to try and prevent activities such as terrorism, human trafficking and drug smuggling from crossing international boundaries. Intelligence agencies from all over the world, such as MI6 and the Federal Bureau of Investigation, regularly work together to share intelligence and information on illegal activities and suspected terrorists in order to increase security in their home countries.

Learning link

To find out more about MI6, look at Chapter 47.

The three international alliances that we will study are:

- the European Union
- NATO
- the United Nations

Show your understanding

1. What is the purpose of international alliances?
2. What methods do economic alliances use to make trading easier between member countries?
3. Describe an example of a successful economic alliance that the UK has recently formed with another country.
4. What are the aims of security alliances?
5. Why do intelligence agencies, such as MI6 and the FBI, often share information with each other?

Collect a skill

Imagine

Imagine you work undercover as a secret agent for an intelligence agency, such as MI6 or the FBI. What sort of things do you think the job would involve? Write about a day in the life of an intelligence agent. You can even research the role of an intelligence agent on the Internet to help you do this.

Activate your brain cells!

Think about it. What problems might NATO's 'an attack on one country is an attack on all' policy cause?

Intelligence agencies such as MI5 (bottom) and the FBI (top) often work together to deal with international security concerns

34 What is the EU?

By the end of this section you should be able to:

▶ Explain why the European Union (EU) was set up

▶ Identify how EU membership benefits EU citizens

▶ Understand how the EU is run

After the end of World War Two, the countries of Europe decided that they must cooperate if they were going to rebuild the trade and industry that had been destroyed and ensure that they never went to war with each other again. This led to six countries (Belgium, France, Germany, Italy, Luxembourg and the Netherlands) signing trade agreements with each other. The UK joined this group in 1973, along with Denmark and Ireland. By 1995, this international alliance had 15 member countries and became known as the European Union (EU). Since then, the EU has enlarged several times and now has 27 members, as well as around 500 million citizens.

What does the EU do?

The EU tries to promote peace and stability for the citizens of all member countries. By doing so, it hopes that it will raise the standard of living for EU citizens and protect their rights.

The EU allows citizens the right to:

- Travel without a visa between member countries with a valid passport
- Study, work or live in another member country without restrictions
- Access consumer goods from other countries easily (e.g. French cheese or Belgian chocolate)
- Use the same currency (the euro) in many of the member countries.

How is the EU run?

The EU is a huge organisation with several parts.

Most big decisions in the EU are made by the **European Council**. Representatives from each of the 27 countries work together to discuss issues which affect them all. Who represents each country depends on what is being discussed. For example, recently many countries have been concerned about a declining honey bee population and the impact that this will have on plant life and honey

1 Austria	15 Latvia
2 Belgium	16 Lithuania
3 Bulgaria	17 Luxembourg
4 Cyprus	18 Malta
5 Czech Republic	19 Netherlands
6 Denmark	20 Poland
7 Estonia	21 Portugal
8 Finland	22 Romania
9 France	23 Slovakia
10 Germany	24 Slovenia
11 Greece	25 Spain
12 Hungary	26 Sweden
13 Ireland	27 United Kingdom
14 Italy	

farming. As this is a farming issue, it has prompted agriculture ministers from all member countries to meet to discuss what should be done about this.

The government of each member state has an opportunity to hold the **Presidency of the Council of Europe**, alongside two other nations, for 18 months. This means that each member state has an opportunity to be part of the presidency every 13.5 years. The UK government will next have this opportunity in 2017, alongside Estonia and Bulgaria. These countries are responsible for chairing European Council meetings. This gives each country an opportunity to set the agenda and bring up issues which are of particular importance to their country.

The **European Commission** organises the day-to-day running of the EU. It suggests Bills (proposed laws) for the European Parliament to vote on, and makes sure that any laws which are passed by the parliament are put in place.

The **European Parliament** decides whether or not the laws proposed by the European Commission should be passed, and it decides how much money the EU should spend. Members of the European Parliament (MEPs) are elected by EU citizens every 5 years. Any EU citizen over the age of 18 years can vote for their MEP. Scotland has six MEPs. How many MEPs each country has

European Parliament, Strasbourg, France

depends on the size of its population. Germany is the largest member country and has 99 MEPs. MEPs are more likely to vote in a united group with MEPs from other countries who share a similar political ideology to pass laws rather than with MEPs from different political parties from their own country. The European Parliament usually meets in Strasbourg, France.

Show your understanding

1. Why was the EU set up?
2. What rights do EU citizens have?
3. What happens at the European Council?
4. What do EU member countries try to do when they have the Presidency of the Council of Europe?
5. What is the relationship between the European Commission and the European Parliament?
6. How do they work out how many MEPs a country has in the European Parliament?

Stretch yourself

Using the list of member countries in the map on page 68, try and find out when each country joined. Try to identify what other countries have applied to join the EU.

35 How does the EU meet the needs of its citizens?

What are we exploring?

By the end of this section you should be able to:

▶ Explain how European Union (EU) economic policies on agriculture and fishing benefit producers

▶ Explain how EU economic policies on agriculture and fishing benefit consumers

The European Union (EU) has many social, economic and political policies which aim to protect citizens and help the economies of member states to grow. These are discussed at the European Council, voted on by the European Parliament and put in place by the European Commission. Any policies made by the EU must be followed by all member states, even if they did not vote for them.

Agriculture and fishing

Agriculture and fishing are two very important industries for EU member states and are strictly governed by EU legislation. The EU has reduced the number of restrictions on trading agricultural products between member states. This means, as

The Common Agricultural Policy protects the rights of farmers in the EU

consumers, we now have access to a much wider range of products from other countries, and at a reasonable price. For example, we can easily buy French cheese or Belgian chocolate in our local supermarket. It also should ensure that the food we eat is of a certain quality and that producers (farmers or fishermen) receive a fair price for their produce. This has been achieved through various economic policies.

The Common Agricultural Policy

The EU also had to consider the problems caused by overproduction of certain agricultural commodities. This has led to the creation of the Common Agricultural Policy (CAP). Overproduction of a product pushes the price that a farmer receives for growing the product down as there is so much of the particular product available for the retailer to buy. For example, before the CAP, it was costing dairy farmers more to produce a litre of milk than retailers were prepared to pay for it.

In the past it has also led to huge amounts of particular products going to waste. This led to what is known as a surplus. In the early 1990s, these surpluses were often referred to as 'grain mountains' and 'wine lakes'. To stop this, the CAP imposed quotas on farmers. This meant that farmers were limited in how much they could grow or produce and this eventually led to less waste and increasing prices. The price that farmers receive from retailers for some products, such as milk, is sometimes subsidised by the EU to ensure they receive a fair price. Some farmers are even paid not to grow anything on certain parts of their land to prevent overproduction.

The Common Fisheries Policy

The fishing industry in member countries is also carefully managed by the EU. The sea around the coastlines of member countries does not have easily controlled borders. This can often lead to disputes when fishing boats from one member state are fishing in waters close to another member state. Fish stocks in EU waters are dwindling, as often fish are caught at a faster rate than they can reproduce. The EU regulates fishing through the Common Fisheries Policy (CFP). This regulates how much fish a country is allowed to catch, where boats are allowed to fish, what size of nets they can use, and what type and size of fish they can catch.

The CFP is regulated through organisations such as the Scottish Fisheries Protection Agency. They monitor fishing all around the Scottish coastline and frequently check that boats only have on board the nets, as well as the type and quantity of fish, that they are allowed by EU law. Agency officers are allowed to board any fishing boat in Scottish waters, regardless of where it is from. There are very serious penalties for any boats breaking their permit, including heavy fines and prison sentences.

? Bore your friends...

Spain and Portugal are the EU countries that consume the most fish, an enormous 40–60kg per head of population each year.

surplus: extra produce that is not needed

Activate your brain cells!

Class discussion: What is a subsidy? Do you agree with subsidies being given to farmers for their produce? What alternatives could there be to subsidies?

Remember to take it in turns to talk, and listen respectfully to other people's opinions, even if they are not the same as yours!

The Common Fisheries Policy is enforced by agencies such as the Scottish Fisheries Protection Agency

Show your understanding

1. Why are EU policies sometimes a problem for member states?
2. In what two ways have EU agriculture and fishing policies benefited consumers?
3. How have EU agricultural and fishery policies benefited producers?
4. What problems are caused by overproduction of agricultural produce?
5. What three methods have the CAP used to try to reduce these problems?
6. What problem does the fishing industry in the EU face?
7. What limits have the CFP placed upon fishermen to try to reduce these problems?

What are we exploring?

By the end of this section you should be able to:

▶ Explain how the human rights of European Union (EU) citizens are protected

▶ Form an opinion on whether prisoners in EU member states should have the right to vote

In addition to protecting the economic rights of European Union (EU) citizens and businesses, the EU also has many policies to protect the social and political rights of EU citizens and businesses. One of the most important agreements that all member states, even new ones, are obliged to abide by is the European Convention on Human Rights (ECHR).

The ECHR was written in 1950 and based on the Universal Declaration of Human Rights. Its main aim was to make sure that many of the atrocities that were committed during World War Two, particularly the Holocaust, would never happen again within Europe.

Although these are human rights that are protected by the EHCR, there are still often cases where citizens may feel that the government of their country is denying them a particular right. If they cannot come to an agreement with their government over a particular right, then citizens can take their government to the European Court of Human Rights in Strasbourg. It is then up to the court to decide whether or not the member state is guilty of denying its citizens rights according to the ECHR.

European Court of Human Rights, Strasbourg, France

What rights do the ECHR protect?

- Right to life.
- Freedom from torture.
- Freedom from slavery and forced labour.
- Right to a fair trial.
- Right to respect privacy and private family life.
- Right to education.
- Right to free elections.

The case of prisoners' voting rights in the UK

In the UK a prisoner took the UK government to the European Court of Human Rights because he felt it was against EU human rights legislation that prisoners in the UK were denied the right to vote in elections. In early 2011, the European Court of Human Rights agreed with convicted murderer John Hirst and demanded that the UK change the law to allow prisoners the right to vote. The UK government was very unhappy about this decision, but has been forced to consider changing its law or faces having to pay British prisoners millions of pounds in compensation. There are only eight other countries in the EU which ban prisoners from voting outright, whereas Germany actively encourages prisoners to vote.

Many people feel strongly that prisoners should not have the right to vote because they have broken the law, and therefore they should have no right to say how the country is governed while they are detained for their crime. However, there is a strong argument that prisoners still should be allowed to vote because they are still subject to the legislation that the government passes, so should have an opportunity to influence it. There is no evidence that denying prisoners the right to vote reduces crime, and many people feel it alienates them even further from society and makes them more likely to re-offend.

Ex-prisoner John Hirst took the UK government to court over prisoners' voting rights

Collect a skill

Justify a point of view

It is important when you express your opinions that you try to give reasons to explain your point of view.

Do you think prisoners in the UK should be allowed to vote? Give reasons to justify your opinion.

Bore your friends...

There are over 25,000 EU laws that affect the UK.

Show your understanding

1. Why was the European Convention on Human Rights created?
2. What can EU citizens do if they believe their government is denying them rights protected by the ECHR?
3. Why does the UK government have to change the law on prisoners voting rights?
4. What are main the arguments against allowing prisoners in the UK to vote?
5. What are the arguments for allowing prisoners in the UK to vote?

37 What does NATO do?

What are we exploring?

By the end of this section you should be able to:

▶ Explain why the North Atlantic Treaty Organization (NATO) was created

▶ Identify how NATO's role has changed in recent years

▶ Describe some of the work which NATO does

The North Atlantic Treaty Organization (NATO) is a military alliance which was set up in 1949 as a response to the expansion of the Soviet Union after World War Two into Eastern European countries, where it was setting up communist governments. This period, known as the Cold War, lasted over 40 years. Many Western European countries feared communism and joined together with the USA to form NATO. It was designed to be a combined military force which could equal the Soviet Union's enormous military resources if the need ever arose. However, the Soviet Union collapsed in 1991 and at that time it looked like NATO no longer had a purpose.

The changing role of NATO

It became apparent after the events of September 11, 2001, when two hijacked aircraft were piloted into the World Trade Center in New York City and one into the Pentagon (US military headquarters) near Washington DC, that Western democracy was facing a new threat: terrorism. The UK and the USA thought that the government in Afghanistan was allowing al-Qaeda, the terrorist group responsible for these attacks, to train its soldiers in their country. This led to the USA and the UK attacking Afghanistan, with the support of NATO.

The leaders of NATO made a decision in 2002 that they would make NATO's new role to provide peace and security for its member countries by combating the new threats that they face from terrorist groups and weapons of mass destruction. NATO now has 28 members, including many former Soviet states, and has invited more to join in the future to work together against the growing problem of terrorism. It also now works in partnership with Russia, its former enemy, against the threat of terrorism.

When the member states of NATO combine their military resources, they have a huge wealth of expertise and advanced military technology at their disposal. These resources have been used in many ways throughout the last 10 years.

NATO troops in action

Gulf of Aden

Afghanistan – after September 11

NATO has provided surveillance aircraft to help find safe routes for soldiers on the ground in Afghanistan since 2003.

Over 130,000 troops from NATO member states are currently working in Afghanistan as part of the International Security Assistance Force (ISAF).

ISAF troops are working to train Afghan police and security forces, as well as provide security for Afghan civilians.

NATO is helping to rebuild infrastructure (roads, bridges, sanitation) that has been destroyed during the conflict.

Somalia – combating piracy in the Gulf of Aden

Many large cargo ships have been hijacked off the east coast of Africa by Somalian pirates over recent years, who are seeking huge ransoms for the safe return of ships and crews.

NATO naval forces and air support are being used to attempt to deter and prevent attacks in this area.

In their first 6 months of deployment in 2009, there were no successful pirate hijacks in the Gulf of Aden.

The level of piracy in this area has since increased. NATO is now trying to capture pirates so they can be brought to justice in the countries of the ships they attack.

NATO support is now focused on ensuring safe passage for humanitarian aid and ships supplying food to poor nations in Africa.

Show your understanding

1. Why was NATO created?
2. Why did NATO have to find a new role after 1991?
3. What is NATO's new focus?
4. What type of contribution have NATO forces made in the Afghanistan conflict?
5. How is NATO assisting in the Gulf of Aden?

Explore further

Research why piracy has become a major problem off the coastline of Somalia.

Bore your friends...

Over 140,000 soldiers have been deployed to Afghanistan under NATO guidance.

38 What does the United Nations do?

By the end of this section you should be able to:

▶ Explain why the United Nations (UN) was set up
▶ Understand how the UN Security Council works
▶ Describe the UN's peacekeeping actions in Libya

The United Nations (UN) is an organisation that aims to provide a forum for countries around the world in which to work together to promote peace and security across the world. Only three of the world's 195 countries are not members, although the extent to which member countries participate in UN actions varies. The UN began in its current form in 1945, with 50 members, in order to try and provide a means of avoiding another world war.

The UN has it headquarters in New York City, but has a presence of some kind in most countries across the world. Its work is divided into two key areas, peacekeeping and humanitarian.

The United Nations' peacekeeping work

The UN tries to prevent the outbreak of conflict between two or more countries, and civil war within a single country. The UN's peacekeeping work is controlled by the Security Council. The Security Council has 15 members. Five members of the Security Council are permanent because they played a major role in setting up the UN and they have the largest armed forces. These countries are China, France, Russia, the UK and the USA. The other 10 members are elected to the Security Council for 2-year terms. The Security Council votes on any action which it thinks should be taken to promote peacekeeping. It takes nine votes to pass a motion proposed at the Security

Council, although if any of the five permanent members votes against it, it will not go ahead. This is called 'veto power'.

The UN has been involved in many conflicts, and often provides military forces from member countries to try and support and promote peace in areas of conflict. Soldiers who are acting on behalf of the UN wear distinctive blue UN berets. This is supposed to show that they are not involved in the conflict and are only there to promote peace. The UN Security Council has many actions it can take to try to prevent war.

The United Nations in Libya

In January 2011, conflict erupted in Libya when rebel forces staged an uprising against the long dictatorship of Colonel Gaddafi in Libya. Many citizens of Libya protested against Gaddafi and demanded democracy. As a response to this, Colonel Gaddafi

- **Promoting peace talks:** The UN encourages groups in conflict to come to a peaceful agreement before conflict worsens.

- **Demand a ceasefire:** Try to persuade the groups/countries in conflict to stop fighting, and patrol this using UN soldiers.

- **Economic sanctions:** The UN asks member states to agree to stop trading with the country in order to try to persuade it to end the conflict.

United Nations Security Council actions to prevent war

- **Military action:** The UN sends in soldiers to try to protect civilians and put other military forces in the area out of action in order to try to bring the conflict to an end.

- **Arms embargo:** The UN asks member countries to stop selling arms and munitions to a particular country, which cuts off valuable supplies which are used in war.

turned his own army on protestors, ordering them to kill anyone against his regime. The UN Security Council's 15 members voted unanimously in February 2011 to enforce an arms embargo and freeze any money which Colonel Gaddafi held overseas in order to prevent him from accessing any new weapons to attack his citizens with. Gaddafi continued his attack on anti-government protestors, so the UN enforced a no-fly zone across this country in order to weaken Colonel Gaddafi's air force. The UN no-fly zone was patrolled by North Atlantic Treaty Organization (NATO) forces. NATO often provides the military resources to carry out any resolutions made by the UN Security Council.

Conflict in Libya

Show your understanding

1. Why was the UN created?
2. Describe how the UN Security Council works?
3. Describe three actions that the UN Security Council can take in order to try to prevent conflict.
4. Why did the UN Security Council decide to take action in the Libyan conflict?
5. What role does NATO sometimes play in UN Security Council actions?

Stretch yourself

Find out which three countries are not members of the UN and why.

How does the United Nations provide humanitarian support?

What are we exploring?

By the end of this section you should be able to:
▶ Name and describe the work of several United Nations (UN) agencies
▶ Use the Internet to research the work of one UN agency in detail

Humanitarian support is work which protects the human rights of others, provides aid when required and supports the development of a country. Most of the humanitarian work that the United Nations (UN) does is carried out by one of the UN's agencies. Most of the UN agencies are large and powerful organisations in their own right. However, most of the UN agencies rely on UN member states choosing to fund their particular work and find it difficult to persuade countries to provide funding during an economic recession. Many agencies have recently been finding it difficult to raise enough money to carry out their work.

There are several agencies which each have a particular area of focus – here are some examples:

Food and Agriculture Organization

The Food and Agriculture Organization's motto, Fiat panis, translates as 'Let there be bread'

- **Role:** To reduce hunger worldwide by improving food supplies.
- **Methods:** Help farmers improve their farming methods to increase crop yields or avoid drought or crop disease and improve standards of living in rural communities.
- **Example:** Worked with farmers in Burkina Faso to improve farming methods. This has resulted in improved crop yields, a better and more reliable food supply and a better standard of living for people in farming communities.

World Health Organization

- **Role:** To improve health in developing countries and avoid epidemic outbreaks of disease worldwide.
- **Methods:** Provide immunisation programmes in developing nations against killer diseases such as tuberculosis and measles. Monitor disease outbreaks worldwide and implement control measures.
- **Example:** Has run a successful vaccination programme in Ethiopia since 1980 against the six main killer diseases. 50% of the population has been vaccinated over the last 30 years.

United Nations Educational, Scientific and Cultural Organization

- **Role:** To protect sites of educational, scientific, natural and cultural heritage.

- **Methods:** Give natural sites and historical monuments World Heritage status and help support their protection.

- **Example:** Parts of the Old Town in Edinburgh have achieved World Heritage status. Sites such as the Zollverein Coal Mine in the Ruhr, Germany, also have achieved world heritage status as it was felt that the preservation of the site is crucial to educating future generations about the area's industrial past.

Zeche Zollverein, Essen, Germany, a UNESCO World Heritage Site

Collect a skill

Mind mapping!

Learning how to draw mind maps may help you in your school subjects. Mind mapping is a method you can use to help you organise your thoughts. In the middle of your page, draw a circle and write 'UN agencies' inside it. Now draw four lines coming out from the circle. It should look like the diagram below. Use the text to help you write a small amount of information about each of the agencies.

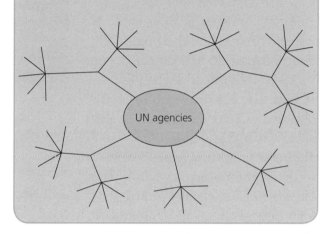

UN agencies

Stretch yourself

Using the Internet, research and prepare a short report on one of the UN agencies mentioned above. Describe some examples of the work they do in other countries.

Show your understanding

1. What is humanitarian work?
2. How does the UN carry out its humanitarian work?
3. How are UN agencies funded?
4. What problems are there with relying on this method of fundraising?

40 What sort of work does UNICEF do?

What are we exploring?

By the end of this section you should be able to:

▶ Describe how the United Nations (UN) protects children's rights

▶ Give examples from Haiti of the type of work that UN Children's Fund (UNICEF) does

A very important United Nations (UN) agency is UNICEF (UN Children's Fund). UNICEF's aim is to protect children and their rights all around the world in accordance with the UN Convention on the Rights of a Child. The UN Convention on the Rights of a Child was created in 1989 because world leaders felt that children under the age of 18 years needed extra special protection. The convention is a legally binding document between all UN member countries.

The Convention has been successful in encouraging countries to include the rights of children in their human rights legislation. However, some countries still do not protect children's rights very well and many of the rights in the Convention are not met.

Across the world, UNICEF works to try and overcome this. Some governments do not agree that children should be entitled to have the rights listed in the Convention. Other countries are too poor to be able to ensure that they protect the rights of child citizens in their country. Sometimes a country may face an event, such as a natural disaster or a war, which prevents citizens from having their basic human rights met. Children are often worst affected in these situations and UNICEF often works in these countries to provide emergency care and long-term support in order to help these children.

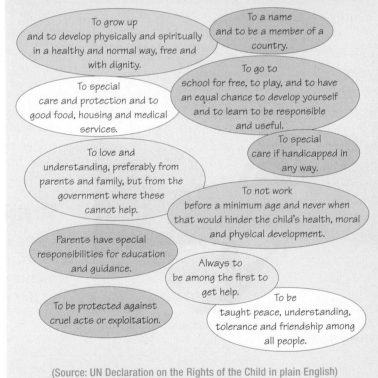

All children are protected by the Convention no matter their race, colour, sex, language, religion, political or other opinion, or where they were born or who they were born to.

Every child has the right:

To grow up and to develop physically and spiritually in a healthy and normal way, free and with dignity.

To a name and to be a member of a country.

To special care and protection and to good food, housing and medical services.

To go to school for free, to play, and to have an equal chance to develop yourself and to learn to be responsible and useful.

To special care if handicapped in any way.

To love and understanding, preferably from parents and family, but from the government where these cannot help.

To not work before a minimum age and never when that would hinder the child's health, moral and physical development.

Parents have special responsibilities for education and guidance.

Always to be among the first to get help.

To be taught peace, understanding, tolerance and friendship among all people.

To be protected against cruel acts or exploitation.

(Source: UN Declaration on the Rights of the Child in plain English)

UNiCEF in Haiti

Background: In January 2010, Haiti experienced a severe 7.0 magnitude earthquake. Approximately 230,000 citizens were killed and a further million were made homeless. Most buildings near the epicentre were not built to withstand an earthquake of this strength, and most of the access to clean water and electricity in this area was severed.

Haiti is a poor country, which already experienced much civil unrest. The government of Haiti relied heavily on support from other countries, charities and international organisations such as the UN to provide emergency aid. It has particularly affected children's rights to be healthy, educated and treated fairly.

The role played by UNICEF: Disease spread quickly because of the high temperatures, high number of dead and lack of access to clean water. Cholera (a diarrhoeal disease) spread quickly through the temporary tented towns, affecting up to 800,000 people. Children are particularly vulnerable to this illness and UNICEF has tried to ensure that children have access to the necessary medication and rehydration salts to recover from this illness.

UNICEF working in Haiti

Additionally, UNICEF has tried to support the 2.5 million children whose education has been interrupted. Of the 4992 schools affected, 80% have reopened as a result of UNICEF's work. Many of these are now tented classrooms. UNICEF has trained 500 health workers to support mothers with newborn babies and to tackle child malnutrition, and has also provided care for the many unaccompanied children whose families are missing or dead.

Show your understanding

1. What does UNICEF stand for?
2. What does UNICEF aim to do?
3. Why was the UN Convention on the Rights of a Child created?
4. Give three reasons why countries often do not protect children's rights.
5. What children's rights were affected by the Haiti earthquake in 2010?
6. Give three examples of ways that UNICEF has tried to improve children's rights in Haiti after the earthquake.

Explore further

The UN has worked in Haiti in both a peacekeeping and humanitarian role for many years. Look up www.un.org to see if you can find out about any of its other work there.

41 What problems do poor countries face?

What are we exploring?

By the end of this section you should be able to:

▶ Describe some of the problems that poor countries may face

▶ Identify whether problems are social, political or economic

Most of the poorest countries in the world are located in the southern hemisphere. Some people refer to the rich north and the poor south. Of course, there are some exceptions to this. Rich countries are often referred to as developed countries.

Poor countries are often referred to as developing countries, because they have a long way to go before they reach the level of wealth that many of the richest countries in the world have.

Lack of food

- Too many people.
- Drought and infertile land.
- For example, the Sahel region in Africa often experiences extremely dry spells, which makes it impossible to grow food and can cause famine.

Drought is a major problem in many poor countries

What are some of the problems that many of the world poorest countries face?

Poor health

- too few doctors and nurses for the population
- healthcare is too expensive for most people
- lack of safe drinking water leads to spread of disease
- spread of HIV/AIDS is a major problem in poorer countries
- one in eight people worldwide have no access to clean drinking water, and 3.5 million people die every year from water-related diseases.

? Bore your friends...

A British person taking a 5-minute shower uses more water than a typical person in a developing country slum uses in a whole day.

41

What help is there for people in need in developing countries?

Poor education

- People cannot afford to send their children to school.
- Females have lower status in many countries and are less likely to be educated.
- Governments do not provide free education.
- The African country of Mali has one of the lowest literacy rates in the world at 26.2%.

Debt

- Repaying loans to other countries prevents governments from investing in services such as health and education.
- People are forced to grow crops to pay off their country's debts rather than feed themselves.
- It is estimated that every debt repayment of $1million made by sub-Saharan African countries causes 24 extra deaths of women during childbirth, and the extra deaths of 159 babies before they reach the age of 1 year old.

War

- Civil wars, leading to huge loss of life.
- Genocide.
- Damage is caused to homes and valuable farmland.
- The number of civilians in 2010 alone killed in the conflict in Afghanistan is 3268.

Poor government

- Some countries have dictatorships, where the leader often puts his own interests before those of his people.
- Many North African countries have recently endured periods of conflict because their leaders are unwilling to have free and fair elections or give up power.

Show your understanding

1. On a blank map of the world, make your own copy of the rich north/poor south.
2. What is a developing country?
3. Take each of the problems listed in the spider diagram. Identify whether it is a social, economic or political problem and place it in the correct column in a table in your jotter.

Social	Economic	Political

4. Which two of these problems do you think are the most serious for poor countries? Explain why.
5. Can you think of any ways that poor countries could be supported to overcome the two problems you have chosen?

42 What is aid?

By the end of this section you should be able to:

▶ Explain the purpose of aid

▶ Describe the different types aid

▶ Understand the difference between good and bad aid

Aid is help given by countries or charities to help those in need. Aid may be given as food, medical supplies, emergency shelters or even in the form of specialist expertise such as doctors or farming experts. The aim of aid is to help communities deal with an immediate crisis that they face in the short term and to help them develop in the longer term.

Aid is given is given by many different groups. Where aid comes from determines what type of aid it is:

- **Bilateral aid:** Aid given directly from one country to another, for example the UK helps provide education facilities in Sudan.

- **Multilateral aid:** Aid given by a group of countries to the receiving country, usually through an alliance such as the European Union (EU) or United Nations (UN). For example, the UN has provided emergency shelters in Haiti after the 2010 earthquake.

- **Voluntary aid:** Aid provided by charities or non-governmental organisations (NGOs). For example, Oxfam has been setting up refugee camps in Liberia to help provide shelter for people fleeing the civil war in the neighbouring Ivory Coast.

Aid can be given in many forms

Aid comes in two main forms:

- **Short-term aid (emergency aid):** This is given to relieve immediate suffering, often in the immediate aftermath of a crisis, such food parcels or emergency shelters after a natural disaster.

- **Long-term aid:** This is given to provide a solution to a long-term problem and help a country or community to develop, such as providing a clean water supply for a village or helping them improve their farming methods to increase crop yield.

Both are equally important in supporting those in need.

? Bore your friends...

The biggest recipient of aid in 2011 was India, although by 2014 it is expected to be Pakistan.

Is all aid good?

Not all aid is good for the countries receiving it. Sometimes rich countries, such as the USA and the UK, provide loans to poor countries to help them provide better services for their citizens. However, loans must be repaid, often with interest, which can push the receiving country into further debt. Pressure groups such as Make Poverty History have campaigned to get the governments of rich countries to cancel the debts that poor countries have with them.

Some rich nations provide 'tied aid' to poor countries. This means the donating country may give the receiving country money to improve their infrastructure, such as their road systems. However, the donating country will insist that the receiving countries buy products or employ contractors from their country to carry out the work, which is often much more expensive than using equipment or labour from the receiving country. Tied aid is controversial, as it often benefits the donating country more than the receiving country. The UK made a commitment to stop giving tied aid in 2001.

Another argument against giving aid is that receiving countries can become reliant on it and then become reluctant to develop. For this reason, self-help schemes are often regarded as the most effective forms of aid to help countries continue to develop. Self-help schemes usually work with local people to teach them how to help themselves in a sustainable way. For example, Oxfam has helped many communities in Tanzania set up building cooperatives. It has taught local men how to make basic and affordable buildings using local materials, and helped them set up businesses to make money from this skill. This means that these communities can now support themselves without aid.

A self-help scheme in action

42

What help is there for people in need in developing countries?

Activate your brain cells!

Do you think the UK should give aid to other countries? Discuss with a partner. Give reasons for your opinion.

Show your understanding

1. What is aid?
2. Make a spider diagram to show all of the bodies that give aid.
3. What is the difference between short-term and long-term aid? Give examples to support your answer.
4. What is tied aid, and why do fewer countries give aid in this form these days?
5. Why are self-help schemes often regarded to be the best form of aid?

Collect a skill

Detect exaggeration

'Rich countries never gain anything from providing aid to poorer countries.'

This is the view of Freddie Jones. To what extent has Freddie Jones exaggerated? Give reasons for your answer.

What are non-governmental organisations?

By the end of this section you should be able to:
▶ Describe what non-governmental organisations are
▶ Explain the type of work non-governmental organisations carry out

Much of the aid delivered around the world is provided by non-governmental organisations (NGOs). These are also sometimes known as charities. NGOs do not belong to any country's national government. Bilateral aid is sometimes not welcomed by the receiving country because it is often seen as interference by the donating country. Because NGOs work independently of national governments, they are often considered to be neutral, especially in countries experiencing a humanitarian crisis brought about by war. For this reason, NGOs are often allowed to work relatively freely in many countries where representatives from another country's government would not be allowed.

What type of work do non-governmental organisations carry out?

The International Red Cross is a good example of an NGO that works worldwide. In addition to its work providing emergency aid during humanitarian crises, the Red Cross often plays the role of trying to protect people during armed conflicts and provide care for **refugees**.

Many NGOs, such as the Red Cross, have individuals working with them who have specialist expertise in particular areas, such as providing relief after a natural disaster. This means that they have individuals who are equipped with the skills to provide support in the aftermath of many disasters all around the word, are often able to travel quickly and often have levels of expertise in their particular field which is greater than any individuals in the country where the disaster has taken place. This makes NGOs crucial during most global humanitarian crises. Governments are often willing to work with NGOs or allow them to **mediate** between warring sides in times of conflict.

refugee: a person who has been forced to leave their country in order to escape war, persecution or natural disaster

mediate: negotiate between groups in dispute

43

What help is there for people in need in developing countries?

What problems do NGOs face?

Most NGOs rely on charitable donations from the general public to raise the money they require for their work. NGOs often find it difficult to raise enough money to cover the costs of their work, particularly in times of recession when people or businesses are less willing to make charitable donations. This can limit the amount of aid they are able to provide.

Also, although NGOs are often viewed as neutral and are able to work relatively freely in many conflict zones, NGO workers are still at risk and sometimes find themselves in dangerous or hostage situations. Scottish aid worker Linda Norgrove died in September 2010 when US armed forces tried to rescue her after she was kidnapped during work with an NGO in Afghanistan. Thousands of aid workers put their lives on the line every day to carry out their work.

Activate your brain cells!

What are the different methods used by NGOs to fundraise. Write a list with a partner.

NGO worker Linda Norgrove was kidnapped in Afghanistan and died during the attempt to rescue her

Show your understanding

1. What are NGOs?
2. Why do NGOs often find it easier to carry out aid work in receiving countries than aid workers sent by the government of another country?
3. List three examples of the type of work that the Red Cross carries out.
4. What are the advantages of NGOs providing aid?
5. What are two main problems that NGOs face?

Bore your friends...

The International Red Cross has over 100 million members, volunteers and supporters worldwide, and has a presence in 187 countries.

Learning link

Try to find out more about the history of the Red Cross and what work it is currently involved in by looking at its website (www.ifrc.org).

44 How does Merlin help people in need?

What are we exploring?

By the end of this section you should be able to:

▶ Explain how Merlin supports people in developing countries

▶ Using the Internet, research the work of Merlin further

Merlin is a UK-based charity which provides specialist medical help in many poorer countries around the world. It was started in 1993 by three friends who managed to organise essential food and medicines worth £1 million to be sent to war-torn Bosnia. Since its small beginnings, Merlin has grown into a much larger charity and has worked in 39 different countries providing medical aid.

Merlin supports countries and communities which are experiencing a medical crisis in two ways. Firstly, it provides emergency medical aid to help countries that may be affected by a crisis such as a natural disaster or war and deal with immediate health issues such as injuries and disease. Secondly, it provides long-term support for countries to help them improve general health, using methods such as ensuring that there are adequately equipped healthcare centres, training local doctors and nurses, and providing health education programmes.

Learning link

Access the Merlin website at www.merlin.org.uk. Find out about the work Merlin does in another country, and prepare a short presentation on this work for the rest of the class.

What does Merlin do in the Democratic Republic of Congo?

The Democratic Republic of Congo (DRC) is a Central African country which was involved in a 5-year-long war with neighbouring states between 1998 and 2003, leaving the country with a major humanitarian crisis. The country is still experiencing pockets of conflict in many parts and it is thought that the war has claimed as many as 3 million lives as a consequence of injuries directly associated with the fighting and disease.

Merlin has been working in the DRC since 1997. It initially provided emergency medical aid to refugees displaced by the fighting in the east of the country. Since then, Merlin has focused on improving general health levels in the areas worst affected by the conflict through supporting and helping rebuild the health system. In 2010, Merlin was supporting approximately 200 medical facilities and nine hospitals, as well as training local medical staff and ensuring better access to medical care for all. It has also ensured access to safe drinking water for over 78,000 people, which has helped reduce the spread of water-borne diseases such as cholera.

Jo Reid, age 28 years, role with Merlin: Programme Assistant in Kindu, Maniema province, DRC.

What made you want to work for an NGO?

I always wanted a job that would allow me to see the world and to give something back at the same time – I never saw myself as being able to do a '9 to 5' office job like most of my friends. I also wanted a job that would be challenging, varied and exciting.

What work do you do with Merlin in the DRC?

In Kindu, our Merlin team carries out health programme activities in support of 54 health facilities across four 'health zones' in central Maniema for the benefit of 500,000 people. My work is to help ensure that these activities are carried out efficiently and effectively. My responsibilities include helping to coordinate the medical, logistics, finance and administration teams (65 staff), monitoring project progress, writing reports, carrying out financial, human resource and administrative management tasks, representing Merlin to our donors, partners and beneficiaries, and supporting emergency response activities, as and when needed.

What do you most enjoy about your work?

I love the fact that from one day to the next I might be doing completely different tasks – from planning training activities with our Congolese partners, to helping to ensure that medicines are delivered to all health centres, to being out in 'the field' supporting a mass vaccination campaign! And I love going out to the health centres we support, some of them in extremely remote areas, and actually seeing the impact of the work we do every day. There is no better job satisfaction than seeing a patient recovering with your own eyes!

What are the biggest challenges you face in your work?

Living and working in remote areas can make even the simplest task much harder, for example just trying to get from A to B in some areas is hard enough after the rains turn the roads into mud and sometimes make bridges collapse. This means we have to plan all activities extremely well in order to avoid the late delivery of medicines and medical supplies to those who need them. And of course working in the Congo basin means it is always hot, humid and full of mosquitoes!

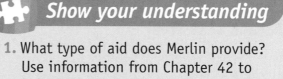

Show your understanding

1. What type of aid does Merlin provide? Use information from Chapter 42 to help you.
2. In what two ways does Merlin help citizens in the countries it works within?
3. What caused the humanitarian crisis in the DRC?
4. How has Merlin helped people in need in the DRC?

44

What help is there for people in need in developing countries?

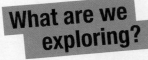

What help is there for people in need in developing countries?

45 What choices can we make to help others?

What are we exploring?

By the end of this section you should be able to:

▶ Understand what it means to be a responsible consumer

▶ Explain why choosing to use Fairtrade products helps support people in poorer nations

Most people are not able to travel to poorer countries to directly help people in need, but there are many choices we can make on a daily basis to help support others. One of the ways we can do this is by being responsible consumers. This means that when we buy a product from a shop, we consider very carefully where it was produced, who it was produced by and what methods were used to produce it. By considering these factors, this can make a very big difference to the lives of the people who produce the things we use on a daily basis. By looking carefully at the labelling of products, we can make decisions about things such as whether or not it is likely that child labour was used in its production and if the producer received a fair price for their work.

The Fairtrade Foundation

The Fairtrade Foundation is a worldwide organisation that was set up to provide a better deal for producers in developing countries and allow them a decent standard of living. It encourages consumers to purchase products that are clearly labelled with the FAIRTRADE Mark. This way, they can be sure that the producer has received a fair price. There are now over 3000 certified Fairtrade products from foodstuffs to flowers and clothing. Look out for the FAIRTRADE Mark on products such as chocolate and fruit juice in the supermarket.

A banana case study

The average banana costs 30p. Who gets what?

Supermarket – 13p

Importer – 5p

Shipper – 6p

Plantation owner – 5p

Worker – 1p

Activate your brain cells!

Class discussion

Think about what things you could do to be a more responsible consumer. Discuss as a class. Remember to listen and take it in turns to speak. It is important that you listen respectfully to other people's opinions, even if they are different to yours.

In most banana-producing countries, the workers who cut down the bananas from the trees often earn very little. On the island of St Vincent in the Caribbean, many workers on the banana plantations earn less than £1 per day, which is barely enough to feed their families. The farmers on St Vincent who produce Fairtrade bananas receive much more than this. Fairtrade producers are also encouraged to use far fewer chemicals that endanger the health of workers and damage the local environment.

The UK started selling its first Fairtrade bananas in 2000. Now 20% of all bananas sold in the UK are Fairtrade. Many shops such as Scotmid now offer a huge number of products for responsible consumers. All you have to do is read the label before you buy to make sure. Fairtrade products sometimes cost a few pence more than other alternatives, but this is usually because the producers are getting a little more money. Some towns and businesses in the UK have now achieved Fairtrade status because of the level of their commitment to using Fairtrade products.

Show your understanding

1. What is a responsible consumer?
2. What are the aims of Fairtrade?
3. How can you be sure that the producer has received a fair price for his work when you buy a product?
4. What two things have improved for workers on plantations that produce Fairtrade bananas on St Vincent?
5. What evidence is there that Fairtrade products are becoming more popular in the UK?

Collect a skill

Calculating percentages
Percentages are just a way of expressing a fraction with a denominator of 100. For example, instead of saying that someone ate ¼ of the cake, you could say that they ate 25% of the cake.

To calculate a percentage you divide the given amount of something by the total amount, and then multiply by 100.

% = given amount/total amount × 100

Work out what percentage each person receives from the sale of a banana. You might need a calculator to help you.

Bore your friends...

The banana is the most popular fruit in the world. People spend over £10 billion per year on bananas worldwide.

Stretch yourself
Conduct a class survey on who uses Fairtrade products at home. Your results can be presented in a table, a graph or a pie chart.

45

What help is there for people in need in developing countries?

Why did the events on September 11, 2001 change the world?

What are we exploring?

By the end of this section you should be able to:

▶ Understand what terrorism is
▶ Explain what impact September 11, 2001 had on the global community

Terrorism is an act of violence that aims to create fear and often inflict injury or death upon its recipient. Terrorist acts are usually carried out to try and achieve a political or a religious goal.

On September 11, 2001 a series of highly organised and coordinated terrorist attacks took place in the USA, when 19 terrorists hijacked four airliners. Three of these were crashed into high-profile buildings, two into the World Trade Center in New York and one into the Pentagon (US military headquarters), and another crash landed in Pennsylvania, although it was believed to have been intended for the Capitol Hill where US Congress sits. Almost 3000 victims from all across the world died, making it the largest loss of life ever from a terrorist attack, with a truly global impact.

The al-Qaeda terrorist network claimed responsibility for this deadly attack, and although it has been responsible for many smaller attacks in the past, this was on a far greater and more organised scale than anything ever witnessed before.

Airliners were flown into the World Trade Center on September 11, 2001

The September 11, attack was a protest against the US military's involvement in many Muslim states. These events signalled to many countries that large-scale threats to their security were no longer likely to come from other nation states, but from sophisticated, well-organised and unpredictable global terrorist networks. Countries such as the USA and UK knew that they were going to have to learn to adapt their security mechanisms to deal with this emerging threat.

What is al-Qaeda?

Al-Qaeda is a global terrorist network which has been in operation since the late 1980s. It describes its cause as a holy war against anti-Islamic forces, which it believes many Western governments are. Its members are often described as 'Islamic extremists' because of the extreme nature of their beliefs, which most certainly do not reflect the opinions of the Muslim faith as a whole. They operate under the leadership of Osama bin Laden. In May 2011, bin Laden was killed by US troops.

Al-Qaeda is a global network, with a presence in many countries across the world. It has no claims to belong in any one country. Individuals operating on behalf of al-Qaeda have often been trained at one of its extensive training camps around the world, such as in Afghanistan. It is well known for its use of suicide bombings and multiple bomb attacks on several targets at once.

Since September 11, 2001, there have been numerous other al-Qaeda-linked acts of terrorism in Western countries.

Osama bin Laden

On 7 July 2005, four al-Qaeda suicide bombers detonated explosives during the rush hour in London across various parts of the public transport system. These attacks left 52 dead and a further 700 injured. The fact that another devastating terrorist plot was successful, despite huge amounts of work by intelligence agencies and increased security, signalled to the UK, USA and many other Western democracies that the threat of extremist groups causing huge destruction is here to stay. Al-Qaeda operatives organise themselves discreetly and their tendency to use suicide bombers makes them incredibly difficult to track and stop. This has forced Western governments to work together in order to reduce the threat of terrorism within their borders.

Show your understanding

1. What is the aim of terrorism?
2. Describe what happened on September 11, 2001.
3. Why did the September 11 attacks change the way that Western governments organise their security?
4. Why has al-Qaeda attacked the USA and UK?
5. Why is the al-Qaeda terrorist network proving difficult for Western governments to stop?

47 Why does the UK government have to work overseas to tackle terrorism?

What are we exploring?

By the end of this section you should be able to:

▶ Explain why the UK government works overseas in order to tackle terrorist threats to the UK mainland

▶ Describe what methods it uses

The UK is no stranger to acts of terrorism. It has been subject to several hundred terrorist attacks since the 1970s, carried out by a number of different terrorist organisations. In fact, the threat of attacks from Islamic extremists is a relatively new one. Most of the terrorist attacks that took place through the 1970s, 1980s and the early 1990s were in fact carried out by the IRA (Irish Republican Army) in protest at the British rule of Northern Ireland, until a **ceasefire** was put in place in 1994. A huge number of explosive devices were planted in British cities over a 25-year period, causing the loss of 115 lives.

> **ceasefire**: all sides in a conflict agree to stop attacking each other

Over the last 40 years, the UK government has worked continuously to try to adapt its **counter-terrorist strategies** in order to deal with new threats and prevent increasingly sophisticated terrorist plots. Most threats to the UK mainland actually originate overseas, which has meant that the UK government also must work overseas in order to reduce the threat of terrorism. It does this in several ways.

> **counter-terrorist strategies**: tactics adopted by government, the amed forces, the police and companies in response to threats from terrorists

Learning link

Try to find out more about the history of the conflict over the governance of Northern Ireland, and why this has resulted in terrorist actions taking place within the UK.

Targeting the root of terrorism in other countries

The British armed forces are deployed in several countries in order to try and target potential terrorist activity before it arrives on British soil. British troops have had a presence in Afghanistan since 2001, as the government has always believed that al-Qaeda has a strong base there. The UK worked alongside other nations in order to try and improve human rights for Afghan citizens and try to reduce the influence of the former Taliban-led government, which was allowing al-Qaeda to base itself and train terrorists within the country. Involvement in the war in Afghanistan has cost the lives of over 350 British soldiers. Many of these have been caused by soldiers detonating improvised explosive devices, which are becoming increasingly difficult to detect. Because of the enormous death toll, support from British citizens for continued involvement in Afghanistan is declining and the UK government may soon be forced to make difficult decisions about the continued deployment of its troops there.

The Taliban supported al-Qaeda in Afghanistan

However, al-Qaeda is an extensive network with a strong presence in several countries across the world, particularly in many North African and Middle Eastern countries and Pakistan. This has meant that the UK government (through agencies such as MI5 and MI6) works with the governments of countries all across the world in order to try and gather information about al-Qaeda's operations and try to reduce its influence, access to weapons (particularly **weapon of mass destruction**) and ability to organise.

weapons of mass destruction: weapons designed to cause huge amounts of damage, such as nuclear bombs

Show your understanding

1. How has terrorism affected the UK over the last 40 years?
2. Why does the UK have to work overseas to try and prevent terrorist attacks taking place within the UK?
3. What is the purpose of British troops being deployed in Afghanistan?
4. Why is British troop deployment in Afghanistan unpopular with many British citizens?
5. Why has the UK government had to move its operations outside Afghanistan to try to combat the threat of al-Qaeda?
6. What role does MI5 play in preventing terrorism?

What are MI5 and MI6?

MI5 and MI6 are the agencies of the UK government that are responsible for protecting the national security of the UK from acts of terrorism and inappropriate actions of other countries. MI5 focuses on domestic surveillance and MI6 works overseas. Almost three-quarters of their work is focused on investigating international terrorism. They both gather most of their information using agents who work secretly, as they believe that this is the most effective way of gathering information, taking action and protecting national security actions. For this reason, together they are often referred to as the 'Secret Service'.

Bore your friends...

The fictional character, James Bond, is an MI6 agent.

48 What is cybercrime?

What are we exploring?

By the end of this section you should be able to:
▶ Explain what cybercrime is
▶ Describe how the UK government tries to prevent cybercrime

The term 'cybercrime' refers to any type of criminal activity that involves a computer and a **network**. Cybercrime is becoming increasingly common as more and more people use the Internet as their main form of communication, and services and businesses become more reliant upon computer networks as part of their operations. It is estimated that cybercrime costs the UK government, business and personal users £27 billion per year in cleaning viruses from computers and in stolen data.

Governments worldwide are now increasingly worried about the potential for terrorists to plot and carry out attacks using the Internet. Terrorists have the potential to bring down entire computer systems of government departments or transportation networks, leaving the UK in a state of chaos. The UK government considers cyber attacks by terrorists to be one of the biggest threats to the UK currently and has invested £650 million in to a new National Cyber Security Programme in order to try and prevent an attack of this kind.

> network: collection of computers or servers which allow flow of data and sharing of information between them

Cybercrime takes many forms and affects people in several ways.

We will look at just a few methods of cybercrime.

Viruses

Viruses are computer programs which 'infect' a computer or computer network. They have many purposes, including preventing your computer from working correctly or allowing others to access your computer and steal personal information. Because they are usually contracted by downloading infected content from the Internet, they can usually be prevented or controlled by having up-to-date anti-virus software installed and avoiding any websites or emails from people or organisations you do not trust.

Fraud

We tend to give a lot of personal information away over the computer through activities such as online shopping, online banking and social networking on sites such as Facebook and Twitter. Sometimes this information can be stolen because a website has had a breach of security and has been hacked. Our personal information can sometimes be used to obtain access to our bank accounts or create false identification for other people. In April 2011, Sony announced that online PlayStation gamers had been subject to a security breach on the server they used. The personal details of 70 million users had been obtained, including email addresses and bank account details.

Cyber bullying

Cyber bullying is when the Internet is used to support the persecution of an individual or group of people. It has particularly become a problem amongst groups of young people. Insensitive or malicious material is often published on social networking sites. It can be something as simple as a nasty comment about someone else, yet can cause a great deal of emotional pain to those whom it victimises. Organisations such as Bullying UK are now specifically targeting cyber bullying as it has become such a huge problem.

Even games console users have recently been affected by cybercrime as online gaming becomes more common

Downloading pirated material

One of the most common types of cybercrime is the downloading of files which the user has not paid the rightful owner for, such as movies and MP3s. It is estimated that 7 million Internet users in the UK illegally download files on a regular basis. This denies artists the revenues they have the right to obtain from their work. Internet service providers, such as Virgin Media, are becoming increasingly tough on this crime and are cutting of Internet access and even using legal action against individuals who continually download illegally.

Activate your brain cells!

Think about it. Are you careful about the personal information you give out on the Internet? How much could be found out about you online?

Show your understanding

1. What is cybercrime?
2. Why has the problem of cybercrime grown in recent years?
3. How has the UK Government responded to the problem of cybercrime? Give evidence to support your answer.
4. Which of the different types of cybercrime are the following people most at risk from? Explain the reasons for your answer:
   You
   Your parents
   The Scottish Parliament
5. Many people download music for free from the Internet, which is against the law. Do you agree that this activity should be illegal? Give reasons to justify your opinion.

❓ Bore your friends...

The most common type of cybercrime in 2011 is individuals or companies accepting payment for goods online, which they fail to deliver.

REVIEW

Make a poster explaining to people how they can protect themselves from cybercrime. Use the headings above to help you.

49 How do I write a decision-making report?

By the end of this section you should be able to:

▶ Read text and extract relevant information

▶ Evaluate points of view and make a decision

▶ Provide evidence to support your opinion

▶ Decision-making exercise: should a minimum price be charged for each unit of alcohol?

Background information

In 2010, the Scottish Government put a Bill forward to the Scottish Parliament to introduce a minimum pricing policy on alcohol in Scotland of 45p per unit. The Scottish Government believes that minimum pricing on alcohol would reduce the number of alcohol-related health problems and reduce alcohol-related crime. It would do this by making strong alcohol more expensive to obtain. The Scottish Parliament rejected this Bill by 76 votes to 49 in November 2010; therefore, as yet it has not become a law.

However, even though minimum alcohol pricing has at present been rejected in Scotland, it may be revisited. There are still many arguments for and against the introduction of minimum alcohol pricing in Scotland. These are examined over the next few pages.

Collect a skill

Learning to make decisions is a key skill in both Modern Studies and life. When making a decision on an issue, you should be able to justify your decision using supporting evidence. This exercise will teach you this skill.

Underage and binge drinking is a big problem in Scotland, and the availability of cheap, high-strength alcohol is often blamed

Activate your brain cells!

Carefully read the background information on the minimum alcohol pricing proposals and all of the sources. Think about the importance of each source as you read.

SOURCE 1: What would 45p per unit minimum alcohol pricing mean?

Now	After minimum pricing
4 × 440 ml can of lager = £3.00	£3.75
700 ml bottle of wine = £3.75	£4.20
2 l bottle of cider = £1.20	£3.75
700 ml bottle of vodka = £8.95	£11.95

SOURCE 2: The relationship between alcohol consumption and price

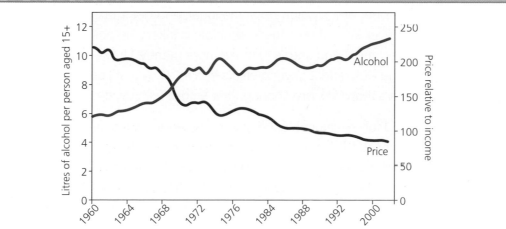

SOURCE 3: Jim Munro, Policy Advisor to the Scottish Government

It is clear that something needs to be done to reduce the level of alcohol-related illness and crime in Scotland. Research has shown that alcohol-related hospital admissions are up 20% over the last 10 years. Alcohol also has a major impact on crime levels in Scotland. Three-quarters of young offenders have been under the influence of alcohol when they committed their crime. The effect of excessive alcohol consumption in Scotland is costing the taxpayer £3.56 billion per year, which could be better spent on other things. 65,000 children per year are also negatively affected by parental alcohol misuse, and it is also a factor in one in three divorces in Scotland. Research has shown that increasing the price of alcohol does tend to lower alcohol consumption levels and that several hundred alcohol-related deaths every year could be avoided as a consequence. It should therefore reduce both health problems and crime levels in Scotland. The extra money generated from minimum alcohol pricing could be put back into the National Health Service (NHS) to help pay for the high cost of alcohol-related illness.

SOURCE 4: Jim Cairns, FastNews Online

Sensible drinkers punished!

The government's proposals to introduce minimum alcohol pricing are a punishment for sensible drinkers. Most people enjoy sharing a bottle of wine with friends occasionally at a dinner party, or a beer and a catch-up at the local, and get a taxi home without causing any trouble whatsoever. Why should these sensible drinkers be penalised – it is just an excuse for the government and shops to make more money. Unlike smoking, sensible drinkers do not negatively affect anyone else's health. They just keep themselves to themselves. Smokers, however, are sharing their smoke with everyone around them.

The levels proposed for minimum alcohol pricing are significant enough to make people a little more out of pocket, but not enough to discourage people from drinking. Many people who drink heavily will just accept increased costs. It will have the effect of those on a low income (who statistically have the highest alcohol consumption rates) being pushed a little bit further into poverty. People who have an alcohol addiction typically use it as an escape. Making alcohol a little more expensive is not a solution for these people. They need money to be spent on proper support to help them reduce their drinking, not more money taken from them!

The only thing you can really do to stop people drinking alcohol is make it more difficult for them to get hold of it. Reducing licensing hours in Scotland has done this. Already people cannot buy alcohol in shops after 10pm, and the opening hours in pubs are now much more tightly controlled. This has done much more to reduce alcohol-related problems than increasing the price ever will.

The Scottish Government should be worrying about the real drug takers. They should be spending more time tackling the growing heroin problem in Scotland. Many heavy drug users turn to burglary and crime to fund their habit, which has a much more serious impact on society than a few people who have had a wee bit much to drink.

By making alcohol more expensive, the Scottish Government is going to increase poverty and, hence, increase the levels of poor health and crime rates. The government must look at alternative solutions, as the current plans to introduce minimum alcohol pricing risk making the gap between rich and poor in Scotland greater than it already is.

SOURCE 5: Scotland's Independent Health 2010 Review

Report

The biggest cause of illness in Scotland is still smoking – 8% of all deaths under the age of 65 are caused by smoking, and 1 in 5 heart attacks are related to smoking. One of the most effective ways to improve general health in Scotland would be to reduce smoking. The Scottish Government has already made excellent progress on this, being the first part of the UK to ban smoking in public places.

However, there are still high numbers of teenagers smoking in Scotland, and the Scottish Government needs to focus on educating young people about the dangers of smoking and providing support to help people quit smoking. Reducing the number of smokers in Scotland is still the single biggest thing that the Scottish Government could do to improve general health, and this should be the main focus of the Scottish Government.

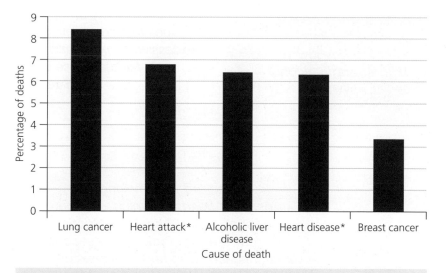

Most common causes of death in those aged under 65 years in Scotland
Source: data from General Register Office for Scotland (2007–2009) figures).
*Usually associated with poor lifestyle, e.g. smoking, excessive alcohol consumption, obesity and lack of exercise

How do I write a decision-making report? *(cont.)*

SOURCE 6: Interviews with people living in Scotland

'I sometimes drink a bottle of cider with my friends at the weekend. We save up our left-over dinner money and buy a bottle between us, because it is really cheap. If it becomes more expensive to buy strong cider, we'll just get something cheaper like wine. I know it has much less alcohol in it, but it is still alcohol.'

Jen, 15

'I never drink cheap wine or lager anyway, so it won't make any difference to me'

Bill, 32

'The rest of the UK is looking seriously at introducing minimum alcohol pricing, so we should be too.'

Bob, 43

'What the government really needs to do is make punishments much more severe for shopkeepers who sell alcohol to teenagers, rather than increase the price. There should be more of a focus on stopping people getting hold of high-strength alcohol.'

Benny, 17

'Minimum alcohol pricing won't penalise sensible drinkers, who tend not to buy low-priced high-strength alcohol anyway.'

Rachel, 29

'On a Friday and Saturday, the majority of the accidents and health issues that come into my A&E are as a result of excessive drinking, and completely avoidable. It is only fair that these people pay for wasting NHS resources.'

A&E doctor

'Scotland has tackled the smoking problem head on, which was the biggest cause of ill health in Scotland. It's now time we took on the second largest health issue and tackle excessive alcohol consumption head on. Minimum alcohol pricing is a positive start in the right direction.'

James McLaren, MSP

Explore further

You could look up information online about the arguments for and against minimum alcohol pricing for use in your report. Remember to write down what your sources of information are, as you will need to refer to this in your report.

Collect a skill

Copy and complete the table below to help you identify all of the arguments surrounding the issue of minimum alcohol pricing in Scotland. Make sure you keep a record of where the information came from. The first one has been done for you.

Arguments for	Arguments against
Research has shown that minimum alcohol pricing reduces alcohol consumption (source 3)	

Imagine you have been employed as a researcher for the Scottish Parliament. It is your job to prepare a report making a recommendation to MSPs on whether or not they should reconsider supporting minimum alcohol pricing in Scotland.

In your report, you must evaluate all sources and write a report summarising all of the arguments on both sides. In your conclusion you must either recommend or reject the proposal to introduce minimum alcohol pricing.

Make sure you explain clearly why you have reached this decision.

Your report should have the following headings.

Introduction: Who are you? What have you been asked to do? Include some background information on the history of minimum alcohol pricing.

Arguments for the introduction of minimum alcohol pricing: Outline the main reasons for your recommendation. Make sure that you use the information from the sources and correctly reference your sources.

Arguments against the introduction of minimum alcohol pricing: Outline the reasons why some people might argue against your recommendation. However, you must try to refute these (give reasons why you think the arguments against your argument are less/not important). This is called a **rebuttal**. Remember, there should always be fewer arguments against your recommendation than for it!

Conclusion: Remember to include reasons to support your decision.

50 What is fast food?

What are we exploring?

By the end of this section you should be able to:
- ▶ Explain what we mean by fast food
- ▶ Understand how the culture of fast food has developed over time

The clue is in the name!

Fast food is the term that we use to describe food that can be prepared and served very quickly. Although in theory anyone can prepare fast food, we normally use the term to describe restaurant food which is packed to take away and includes pre-heated or pre-cooked ingredients.

Activate your brain cells!

In pairs, name as many fast food brands as you can (e.g. McDonald's, Burger King, etc.). How many did you get? As a class, what is your favourite fast food chain?

How long has 'fast food' been around?

A long time is the easy answer to this question. The idea of ready-cooked food for sale has always been very closely connected with urban development. It can be dated back to at least Ancient Rome, where street stands and vendors selling bread and wine were very common.

It is important not to think of fast food as just large restaurant chains (e.g. McDonald's). Street stands are where the concept of fast and convenient food first began, and the type of food varies depending on where you are in the world. For example, street fast food is more likely to include fish if the place you buy it from is close to the sea.

The cultural significance of food

Food is very culturally significant and the types of food served on street-side stands and local restaurants are seeped in the history and the culture of an area.

For example, noodle stands, shops and bars are popular in East Asian cities, flatbread and falafel are everywhere in the Middle East and in India fast food dishes include vadapav and panipuri. New York City is full of hot dog carts, while in the UK, fish and chips remains the nation's favourite.

? Bore your friends...

The term 'fast food' was first recognised in a dictionary in 1951.

The fast food franchise revolution

Although the idea of fast food has been around for a long time, fast food franchises are a fairly new development.

A franchise is when you buy the rights to copy someone else's business model and the rights to use its trademarks, brands and products. It costs quite a lot of money to buy into a franchise but you can normally make your money back because people (consumers) are already familiar with and trust the brand.

In 2010, there were 37,300 partner franchises of McDonald's around the world, and if you wanted to buy into the franchise it would cost you between $995,900 and $1,842,700 (depending on the location of the store).

The history of McDonald's

1940 McDonald's began in 1940, when brothers Richard and Maurice McDonald opened a restaurant in San Bernardino, California.

1948 The McDonald brothers developed the 'Speedee Service System', which established the principles of the modern fast food restaurant.

1949 McDonald's French fries replaced potato chips (chips) on the menu.

1955 McDonald's first franchise was opened in Des Plaines, Illinois, by Ray Kroc (Kroc would later buy the McDonald brothers out of the company).

1958 MacDonald's sells its 100 millionth hamburger.

1967 The company's original mascot, 'Speedee', was replaced with 'Ronald McDonald'. This was also the year the first international McDonald's opened.

1968 The famous McDonald's double arch logo was trademarked and started to be used. This was also the year the 'Big Mac' was introduced.

1975 The introduction of the McDonald's breakfast.

1978 Restaurant 5000 opens in Kanagawa, Japan.

1990 First McDonald's restaurant in Russia opens in Moscow.

1996 McDonalds.com launches.

2003 Premium salads added to the McDonald's menu.

2005 McDonald's celebrates its 50th anniversary on 15 April.

2010 Real fruit smoothies added to the menu.

Show your understanding

1. In your own words describe fast food.
2. What type of street-side fast food do you think would be popular in Japan, Nepal, France, Germany and Brazil? Write your answer as a table.
3. What is a franchise?
4. How much is $995,900–$1,842,700 in GBP?
5. Why do you think a McDonald's opening in your town might be more successful than Mr Smith's Burger Bar?
6. What are falafel, vadapav and panipuri? If no one knows the answer, then use the Internet!
7. Fish and chips is the UK's favourite type of fast food. Do you think this is the same in Scotland? Explain your answer.
8. Why do you think a McDonald's opening in Moscow was such a significant company milestone?
9. Why do you think McDonald's started selling salads and fruit smoothies?

Explore further

Have a look at the interactive timeline of McDonald's history – http://mcd.to/kYvSL

51 Where does our food come from?

What are we exploring?

By the end of this section you should be able to:

▶ Explain what we mean by food miles
▶ Explain why different types of food travel a long way to get to your plate

Although we normally buy food at the local shop or supermarket, very little food in the UK comes from truly local sources. Many products that are out of season in the UK have to travel thousands of miles to get to our shelves. Even food from the UK (particularly if you live in the north of Scotland!) may have travelled hundreds of miles by road or rail.

Food miles (or food kilometres) describe the distance that food is transported as it travels from producer to consumer (the person who eats it). In the UK, it is estimated that our food travels 30 billion kilometres each year.

Activate your brain cells!

Without naming the types of food, describe to a partner what you had for your dinner last night. You are allowed to mention things like colour, shape and taste. See if he or she can guess what you had (do not forget to describe your dessert as well)!

How far does your food travel?

This is a complicated question, because it depends on what you are eating and where you are eating it. But let's pretend that you are chomping into this chicken and bacon burger in a restaurant in Scotland's capital city, Edinburgh.

The chicken comes from a poultry farm in East Lothian – about 20 miles away. So that is not too bad …

But:

- The bacon comes from Denmark – about 600 miles away.
- The bread to make the roll has come from Sheffield – about 190 miles away. But the wheat to make the bread came from Canada and the sesame seeds on top of the bread came from the USA (that is a massive amount of distance!).
- The tomato and cheese come from the south of Italy – at least 1500 miles away. Remember they do not get shipped together – so that is actually at least 3000 food miles!

Cherry Tomatoes
Mouthwateringly sweet. Ideal for snacks and salads or skewered on kebabs

Food facts
✔ Natural source of vitamin C
✔ Naturally high in fibre
WASH BEFORE USE   CLASS 1

Country of Origin:	DISPLAY UNTIL:
SPAIN 13.22	21 JUL
520209	BEST BEFORE:
20/35MM 1807	23 JUL

400g

- The onion comes from France (what a stereotype!) – at least 500 miles away.
- The mushrooms come from Northern Ireland – about 250 miles away.
- The lettuce comes from Devon (in the UK but a long way from Scotland) – about 450 miles away.

Food transport and the environment

Food transport is responsible for the UK adding nearly 19 million tonnes of carbon dioxide to the atmosphere each year. Over 2 million tonnes of this is produced simply by cars travelling to and from shops. Carbon dioxide is one of the gases that contribute to global warming.

Using services like Tesco Direct can contribute to reducing carbon dioxide emissions.

Show your understanding

1. What are food miles?
2. If you could only eat food that was grown locally to you in Scotland, what do you think your main diet would be?
3. Why do you think it is more expensive to buy cheese in a supermarket on Shetland than a supermarket in Glasgow?
4. Look at the picture of the chicken and bacon burger and read the information. How far has it travelled?
5. How does eating fast food (or any food really) contribute to global warming?
6. Why might having food delivered to your door (e.g. by Tesco Direct) actually reduce carbon dioxide emissions compared with driving to the supermarket?
7. Tonight, carefully record the different locations that your dinner has travelled from.
   Use the food miles calculator (link below) to work out how much it cost to get your dinner to you.

Explore further

Here is a nice food miles calculator from Organic Linker. It calculates how much it costs to get food to you, but also the costs of getting waste foods away from you, and to the landfill! http://bit.ly/10jLdN.

52 How much oil does it take to make a sandwich?

What are we exploring?

By the end of this section you should be able to:
- ▶ Explain what actually goes into a sandwich
- ▶ Explain why packaged sandwiches are dripping with oil

The title of this section is not something that you really think about is it?

Have you every wondered how much fossil fuel it takes to make a sandwich? Probably not – but that is what we are going to find out about in this section.

Let's start with a typical sandwich that you might buy from a supermarket or from a petrol station. If you have ever had a sandwich like this you will know that some are better than others!

Now lets focus on the ingredients of this off-the-shelf ham sandwich.

First of all, bread.

Producing bread is a long and complicated process. First of all, somewhere in the world a farmer has had to plant the cereal crops (normally wheat). This is normally done using a diesel tractor, which is used to plough, harrow (prepare) and drill the seeds into the soil.

Then, to protect the crop and help it grow, the farmer needs to add chemicals such as fungicides, pesticides and herbicides. All of these chemicals are made from oil. Nutrients are also added to the crop in the form of chemical fertilisers. Currently, most fertilisers are derived from natural gas.

Once the grain is ready, it needs to be harvested – again normally using a diesel tractor – and then dried using large gas or electric industrial heaters.

Activate your brain cells!

Think about the last really nice sandwich that you ate (or saw someone eat). Make a quick list of all the ingredients within it. Who in your class has eaten the biggest (and probably most environmentally unfriendly) sandwich?

Next the grain has to be driven by diesel lorry to be processed and made into bread, as the type of bread that is manufactured for boxed sandwiches is not produced by hand. It is a huge industrial process.

Next up is the ham (remember it is a ham sandwich).

As you probably already know ham comes from pigs. The production of ham is even more energy hungry than the production of bread. The reason for this is that pigs feed on grain (the same thing bread is made from). An average pig used to produce sandwich ham can eat half a tonne of grain in its lifetime.

Finally, in our ham sandwich we have a little bit of (very tokenistic) salad. This has probably had to be shipped or flown from another country, creating a massive amount of air miles, or grown in a heated greenhouse.

Finally, to produce the sandwich, all of the above ingredients were either cooked or cooled, or both, and then driven mile after mile before they were assembled into a sandwich, after which they would have been packed and driven again to the place where they were going to be sold.

Show your understanding

1. Explain the production of a ham sandwich (or a sandwich of your choice). Include in your answer why it takes a lot of energy to produce a sandwich.
2. Why do we use the term fossil fuel?
3. Why is producing ham more environmentally unfriendly than producing wheat?
4. What do we mean by the word 'tokenistic'?
5. Why do you think that some people describe packaged sandwiches as 'dripping with oil?'
6. Think about the list of ingredients that you put together for the 'activate your brain cells' activity. Write a new list, this time including all the ingredients of a sandwich (e.g. wheat, herbicide, etc.).

? Bore your friends...

Half a tonne is 500 bags of sugar – that is a lot of grain!

Explore further

This 3-minute clip from the BBC tells a similar story very nicely: http://bbc.in/98WRI.

53 Why is fast food a global brand?

What are we exploring?

By the end of this section you should be able to:

▶ Explain what we mean by brands and globalisation
▶ Explain why McDonald's is an example of a global brand

Activate your brain cells!

Without mentioning the name, describe the logo of a fast food brand to a partner. See if he or she can recognise it.

The reason that you can probably recognise so many logos is because of branding. Globally, industries spend billions of pounds each year on branding so that their products are recognised and trusted by consumers (the people who buy their projects).

Many fast food companies (such as the ones in the picture above) are examples of global brands. They operate in lots of different countries around the world and the fast food industry is a good example of globalisation.

What is globalisation?

Globalisation describes the process by which the world is becoming increasingly interconnected. Globalisation is not a new thing but technology, increased curiosity and improved trading relations have really sped things up over the last 50 years.

Trade has been one of the key drivers of globalisation, and many parts of the world now rely on each other to produce goods and maintain their overall standard of living (the chicken and bacon burger on page 106 is quite a good example of this).

When a country is reliant on another country or group of countries, we call this interdependence.

Increased globalisation has resulted in many businesses setting up in other countries, buying operations there or expanding into them. Companies that operate in a number of countries are called multinational companies (MNCs).

McDonald's is an example of an MNC, but there are lots of others as well, such as Shell, Nike, B&Q, Coca-Cola and Ford.

In 2006, the global fast food market grew by 4.8% and reached a total value of $102.4 billion. In India alone the fast food industry is growing at a rate of over 35% a year.

McDonald's: a global industry

McDonald's has over 31,000 restaurants in 126 countries on 6 continents. Its busiest restaurant is in Moscow (which opened in 1990) and its largest restaurant in located in Beijing, People's Republic of China.

More than 75% of McDonald's restaurants worldwide are owned and operated by independent local men and women as franchises (see page 105).

Owing to its brand, McDonald's is instantly recognisable in any of its 31,000 restaurants worldwide. However, despite all of its restaurants having common characteristics, the food is sometimes a little different to satisfy local need.

In India, you will not find Big Macs. Instead you will find a Maharaja Mac, which is similar to a Big Mac but made of lamb or chicken meat.

In parts of Canada, McDonald's restaurants sell a lobster item called McLobster, a lobster roll; the same is sold as McHomard in French-speaking parts of Canada.

In Japan, McDonald's restaurants have introduced the McShrimp, or Ebi Filet-O, to suit Japanese tastes.

In Germany, most McDonald's restaurants sell German beer.

Show your understanding

1. What is a global brand?
2. In your own words explain globalisation.
3. What makes McDonald's a global industry?
4. Look at the various types of McDonald's meal in different parts of the world. Why are they different?
5. Do you get beefburgers in India?
6. Do you think selling beer with fast food is a good idea? Justify your answer.
7. Why do you think McLobster is sold only in parts of Canada?
8. Why is avocado paste more popular than ketchup in Chile?
9. Out of the 31,000 McDonald's worldwide, there is only one that does not use the famous yellow arches. See if you can find out where it is and why it does not use them.

Explore further

Find out all you ever need to know about McDonald's at www.mcdonalds.co.uk.

54 Is Scotland facing a food crisis?

What are we exploring?

By the end of this section you should be able to:

▶ Explain what we mean by a global food crisis

▶ Explain why farming practice and behaviour need to change over the next 50 years

In 2008 and 2010, devastating droughts hit Australia, pretty much destroying its wheat harvest for the year. Although on the other side of the world from Scotland, the consequences of the drought shook the world as global wheat prices increased by 130%, while shopping bills in Scotland and the rest of the UK increased by 15%.

Global warming has been blamed for the droughts in Australia, and many scientists are warning that the worst is still to come, with other similar events occurring around the world. The consequences of increased droughts and the unreliability of the weather has the potential to lead to a global food shortage.

What does this mean for Scotland?

The reliable availability of food that was once taken for granted has become a major cause for alarm among politicians and scientists. The problem is that we do not actually grow a lot of things any more, we have built on a lot of our farm land and we have a growing population. Scotland imports a lot of the food that it eats.

In Scotland, a global food shortage would dramatically increase the import costs of food, making it more expensive. To make matters worse, as import crops start to become more unreliable, farmers in the UK are also starting to feel the impact of disrupted rainfall and rising temperatures.

Activate your brain cells!

Write down as many products as you can think of that are actually grown and eaten in Scotland.

❓ Bore your friends...

Did you know that some Orkney smoked salmon originates from Chile?

Population growth

As well as the complications of growing and importing food created by a changing climate, global population growth is another complicating factor. Over the next 40 years, the UK's population will rise from 60 to 75 million while the world's will leap from 7.0 to 9 billion.

Globally, this means we will have to grow more food on less land, using less water and less fertiliser, while producing fewer greenhouse gas emissions. In fact, population growth means that over the next 50 years we are going to have to produce as much food as we have produced over the past 5000 years!

It gets worse! – increased disease

Farmers over the next 50 years will not only have to improve yields using less fertiliser, but they will also have to develop systems to fight off new agricultural pests and diseases. As global temperatures have risen, more and more devastating varieties of viruses and fungi have spread around the globe.

Scientists think that about 40% of crops in the UK are vulnerable to destruction by weeds, fungi and insects. Livestock is also very vulnerable.

An example of this is bluetongue disease, a virus that affects cattle, sheep, deer and goats and is spread by midges (we have a few of those in Scotland!). The disease was unknown in north-west Europe until 2006, when an outbreak occurred in Holland and spread to nearby countries. In 2007, it spread to the UK, where the authorities managed to stop it.

What can be done?

The simple truth is that there is not really an easy answer to this very complicated and unpredictable problem. Individuals and organisations certainly need to start using less and producing less waste. But if we really want to have a longer lasting impact and a real change, political funding will be needed at the highest level.

'People do not quite realise the scale of the issue. This is one of the most serious problems that science has ever faced. In the UK, the lives of hundreds of thousands of people will be threatened by food shortages. Across the globe, tens of millions, if not hundreds of millions, will be affected.'

Dr Tom Hooper (RothamsteadResearch)

🔍 Explore further

A nice little video and more information on food security – www.foodsecurity.ac.uk.

🧩 Show your understanding

1. Why does a drought in Australia affect food prices in Scotland?
2. Why might Scotland be in trouble if it cannot afford to import food?
3. Why will a rising population also put pressure on food production?
4. Why will there be fewer fertilisers in the next 50 years (page 108 might help remind you of this)?
5. Why is Scotland likely to get more viruses and fungi affecting crops and livestock over the next 50 years?
6. Look at the quote from Dr Tom Hooper above – do you think he is exaggerating? Explain your answer.

55 What happens if you eat too much fast food?

What are we exploring?

By the end of this section you should be able to:
▶ Explain what happens when you eat a poor diet
▶ Explain why being healthier could be good for Scotland

Is fast food good for you?

This is a pretty difficult question to answer as it depends on the type of fast food, the amount you consume and your other lifestyle factors.

However, as a general rule, too much of anything is bad for you and where possible you should try to eat a balanced diet. It is OK to eat fast food as long as you do it in moderation (like anything).

What if you eat too much?

Fast food is normally high in trans-fat content, and studies have found links between the amount of fast food you eat and weight gain.

In 2006, a study on monkeys was carried out in the USA. One group of monkeys were fed a diet consisting of a similar level of trans fats that are consumed when a person eats fast food regularly. The other group were fed a more balanced diet. Both diets contained the same overall number of calories.

The study found that the monkeys who consumed higher level of trans fat developed more abdominal fat (weight) than those who were fed a diet rich in unsaturated fats. They also developed signs of insulin resistance, which is an early indicator of diabetes. After 5 years on the diet, the trans fat-fed monkeys had gained

Activate your brain cells!

Using only mime, describe your favourite McDonald's meal to the person sat next to you.

7.2% of their body weight, compared with just 1.8% in the unsaturated fat group!

Consequences of a poor diet

There are a number of consequences of eating a poor diet, and these are made worse when combined with a lack of exercise. Possible consequences include the following.

Physical consequences

Obesity is when you become clinically overweight. It is caused by a combination of a high-fat diet and a lack of exercise. Obesity can increase the chances of heart disease and strokes. There is also medical evidence to suggest that overweight men run a higher risk of prostate cancer.

Clogged arteries are caused by eating too much fatty food. This increases the risk of heart disease. A high-fat diet can also increase the risk of bowel and stomach cancers. According to the British Heart Foundation, someone has a heart attack in Scotland every 15 minutes.

Diabetes is a condition where the amount of glucose in your blood is too high because the body cannot use it properly. This is because your pancreas does not produce enough insulin. People suffering from diabetes have to control their blood sugar levels by keeping a close eye on their diet and people with some types of diabetes need to take tablets or insulin injections. Diabetes can be fatal if it is not managed properly.

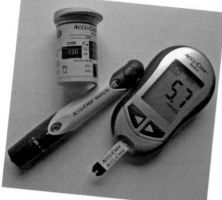

Economic and social consequences

Each year, National Health Service (NHS) Scotland spends over £5 million on prescription drugs to help people tackle obesity. It also spends more vital resources looking after and treating people who are suffering from illnesses brought on by a poor diet.

There are strong links to mental health issues brought on by rapid weight gain.

In 2004, Morgan Spurlock produced and starred in a documentary called *Super Size Me*.

In the film, Spurlock followed a 30-day period in which he ate only McDonald's food. Spurlock dined at McDonald's restaurants three times per day, eating every item on the chain's menu.

"I'm Lovin' it!"
Peter Travers, Rolling Stone

Una película de porciones épicas dirigida por Morgan Spurlock

SUPER SIZE ME
¿Comerías de todo?

As a result of the experiment, the then 32-year-old Spurlock increased his body mass by 13% and experienced mood swings, sexual dysfunction and fat accumulation to his liver. It took Spurlock 14 months to lose the weight gained from his experiment!

Show your understanding

1. Why is 'Is fast food good for you?' a difficult question?
2. Briefly explain what happened in the 5-year monkey experiment.
3. Make a table of the consequences of over-eating.
4. Over-eating and obesity are massive financial drains on Scotland's resources. What could be done to improve the situation and where would you invest the money that you would save?
5. What do you think would happen to you if you ate McDonald's for 30 days?

Explore further

You can watch the full-length Morgan Spurlock 2004 *Super Size Me* film on YouTube: http://bit.ly/yyR5h7.

56 Food and the environment

What are we exploring?

By the end of this section you should be able to:

▶ Explain what we mean by food miles

▶ Explain the ways in which the production of food impacts on the environment

There are lots of ways that food can have an impact on the environment.

Food miles

We have already discussed the environmental impacts of fast food. However, the really interesting thing is that the foods that you should have more of are also the most environmentally friendly. The infographic below displays this well.

How can you do your bit? – Watch what you eat and explain food miles to family and friends.

Activate your brain cells!

List five types of food packaging that is disposed of as soon as the food is eaten. Discuss with a partner how each item has an impact on the environment.

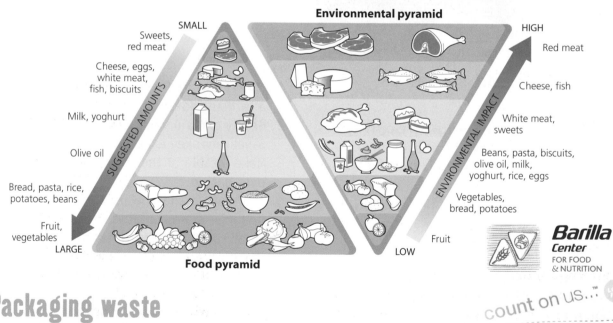

Environmental pyramid

SMALL — Sweets, red meat

Cheese, eggs, white meat, fish, biscuits

Milk, yoghurt

Olive oil

Bread, pasta, rice, potatoes, beans

Fruit, vegetables — LARGE

SUGGESTED AMOUNTS

Food pyramid

HIGH — Red meat

Cheese, fish

White meat, sweets

Beans, pasta, biscuits, olive oil, milk, yoghurt, rice, eggs

Vegetables, bread, potatoes

Fruit — LOW

ENVIRONMENTAL IMPACT

Barilla
Center
FOR FOOD & NUTRITION

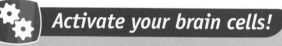

Packaging waste

One of the other byproducts of food (in particular fast food) is excess packaging. According to Waste Online, UK households produce the equivalent weight of around 245 jumbo jets per week in packaging waste.

Many fast food and large supermarket chains now use less polystyrene and more recycled cardboard. However, there is still room for improvement.

Marks & Spencer uses packaging which is less environmentally damaging. The window in the box is also made from biodegradable maize starch and not from plastic.

How can you do your bit? – Be careful what you buy. Put pressure on local shop-keepers to reduce packaging. Re-use plastic bags at the supermarket.

Food waste at home

Research suggests that British people needlessly throw away 3.6 million tonnes of food every year. Salad, fruit and bread are the most commonly wasted food types, and 60% of all dumped food is untouched.

This is the equivalent to about £9 billion worth of avoidable food waste, and, to make matters worse, about £1 billion worth of the food dumped is still in date and the rest is food that could have probably been consumed if it had been better stored or managed or had not been left uneaten on a plate.

How can you do your bit? – Do not be greedy. Plan your meals by best-before date rather than what you want at the time. Freeze food before it goes out of date. Compost any food leftovers.

Food waste out at sea

Around half of the fish caught by fishermen in the North Sea are unnecessarily thrown back into the ocean. The problem is that in a mixed fishery, where many different fish live together, fishermen cannot control the species that they catch.

Fishing for one species often means catching another, and if people do not want them or fishermen are not allowed to land them, the only option is to throw them overboard. The vast majority of these discarded fish will die.

Because discards are not monitored, it is difficult to know exactly how many fish are being thrown away. But the European Union (EU) estimates that, in the North Sea, discards are between 40% and 60% of the total catch.

Other discards are prime cod, haddock, plaice and other popular food species that are 'over quota'. The quota system is intended to protect fish stocks by setting limits on how many fish of a certain species should be caught. Fishermen are not allowed to land any over-quota fish; if they accidentally catch them – which they cannot help but do – there is no choice but to throw them overboard before they reach the docks.

How can you do your bit? – This is a bit more complicated as we need to get the law changed. Join the campaign at www.fishfight.net.

Show your understanding

1. Look at the infographic on page 116. Explain in detail why it is better to eat more fruit and vegetables than cake and red meat.
2. Write a list of food packaging that you have had to throw away in the last week.
3. Why is Marks & Spencer's packaging better than most food packaging?
4. Look at the picture of the rotting food. With thousands of people dying from malnutrition each day, how does that picture make your feel?
5. Explain why fisherman have to throw between 40% and 60% of their total catch back into the sea.

Explore further

To see an interactive infographic of the environmental impact of foods, go to http://bit.ly/dk6KYu.

57 Where would you locate a burger bar?

What are we exploring?

By the end of this section you should be able to:

▶ Explain the location factors for the fast food industry
▶ Know where might you locate a new fast food business in your local town

Just like any industry, the location of the fast food outlet is important for it to generate sales and turn over a profit.

Activate your brain cells!

On a blank piece of paper, draw a cross in the middle to represent your school. Add a north arrow to give you map some orientation. Draw other crosses on your map to represent fast food outlets and their approximate location around your school. Compare and discuss your map with a partner.

For the fast food industry, these location factors include the following:

- What skills people need to be able to manage a restaurant and produce and serve fast food meals.
- Whether there is an appropriate labour supply of people nearby to work in the restaurant/food outlet.
- Whether there is a suitable site to build a restaurant. Is there enough flat land for the building, car park and expansion if necessary?
- Whether the market (customers) is nearby.
- Whether there are good transport links that go past the restaurant to allow people to get there easily and for goods to be easily delivered.
- Whether there is an older restaurant nearby that could just be converted/re-branded to a new branch of a fast food chain. Is any government aid available for this?

People are the key

One of the most important location factors for the fast food industry is being near people. This is one of the reasons that you get fast food outlets inside shopping centres, near cinemas and in out-of-town shopping areas.

Depending on the type of people in these areas, this may also have an impact on the type of food being sold. This is one of the reasons that McDonald's changes its menu at different restaurants around the world (see Chapter 53).

The fast food industry is also highly adaptable and, as well as having fixed locations, it has also developed ways to take food to people. These are normally fast food vans (that move from place to place) or temporary fixtures that you sometimes see at fairs and concerts.

Schools, colleges and universities are also a huge market for the fast food and mobile fast food industry. These are examples of seasonal industries, which means that they are only open for certain times of the day, week or year. For example, it is not uncommon for a fast food outlet to be open outside a school between 11 a.m. and 2 p.m., Monday to Friday, during term time but shut during the rest of the day, at weekends and in the school holidays.

The problems with seasonal business

Although the seasonal fast food business is good for turning over a profit, there are also associated problems for the local community/area. Seasonal business is an example of a high-intensity service industry. This means that it has a lot of customers in a short space of time, which can generate lots of litter, noise and overcrowding.

This can also generate additional problems for schools, which have to sell healthy food inside, yet at the school gates or down the road fast food vendors are allowed to sell whatever they want.

Where would you locate your fast food business?

Think about your school and your local area. Develop a business plan to set up a fast food outlet in your local community. Answer the following questions to help you do this:

- What will you call your business?
- What will be the main products that you sell? Remember fast food restaurants have a small menu (sometimes just one item) that can be produced quickly.
- How much will you sell your products for (you might need to do some research)?
- What other overheads will you need to take into account (packaging, wages, shop rent, insurance)?
- Who will your main market be (how do you know they will buy from you)?
- Where will you locate your industry?
- Who do you need to get permission from to locate your industry in your chosen place?
- Will you be a seasonal or all-year-round industry?
- How will you deal with associated industry problems (e.g. litter, noise, overcrowding)?
- How much profit will you turn over a week, month and year? And how much will go to the tax man?
- What will you do with the profits (spend or reinvest)?
- Design a business and marketing plan to get your business off the ground.

🔍 **Explore further**

This GIS map produced by ESRI shows the location of fast food outlets to secondary schools in south-east Queensland, Australia: http://bit.ly/h4TUHf. The fast food companies say they are not targeting schools (http://bit.ly/eFbJdf). What do you think?

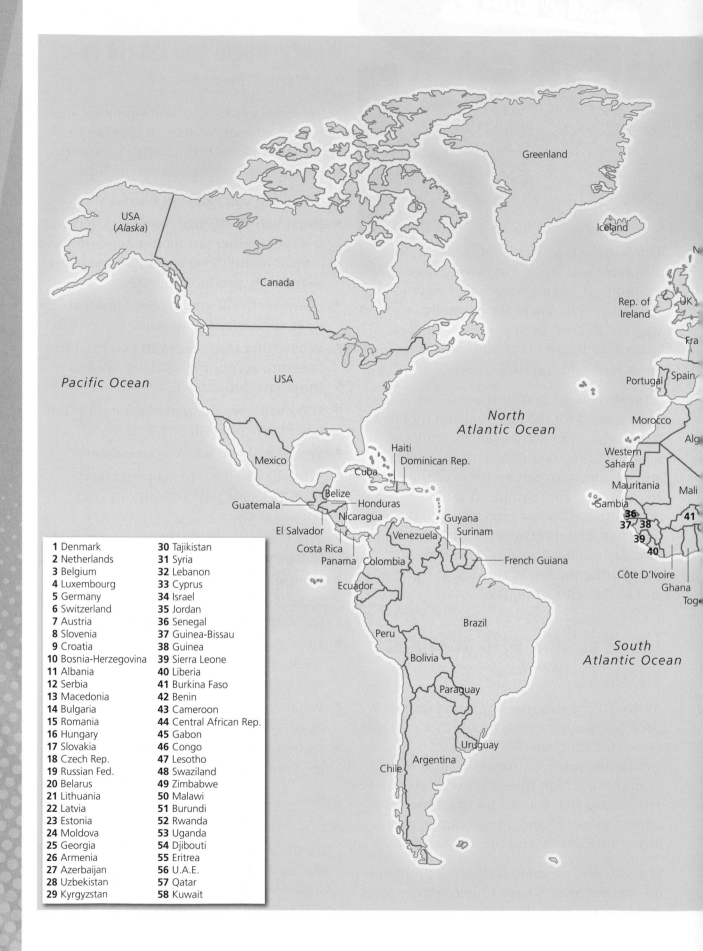

Greenland

Iceland

USA
(*Alaska*)

Canada

Rep. of
Ireland

UK

Fra

Pacific Ocean

USA

Portugal

Spain

*North
Atlantic Ocean*

Morocco

Alg

Western
Sahara

Mexico

Haiti

Dominican Rep.

Cuba

Mauritania

Mali

Belize

Guatemala

Honduras

Gambia

36

41

37 **38**

El Salvador

Nicaragua

39

Costa Rica

Venezuela

Guyana

Surinam

40

Panama

Colombia

French Guiana

Côte D'Ivoire

Ghana

Ecuador

Tog

Peru

Brazil

*South
Atlantic Ocean*

Bolivia

Paraguay

Uruguay

Chile

Argentina

1 Denmark		**30** Tajikistan	
2 Netherlands		**31** Syria	
3 Belgium		**32** Lebanon	
4 Luxembourg		**33** Cyprus	
5 Germany		**34** Israel	
6 Switzerland		**35** Jordan	
7 Austria		**36** Senegal	
8 Slovenia		**37** Guinea-Bissau	
9 Croatia		**38** Guinea	
10 Bosnia-Herzegovina		**39** Sierra Leone	
11 Albania		**40** Liberia	
12 Serbia		**41** Burkina Faso	
13 Macedonia		**42** Benin	
14 Bulgaria		**43** Cameroon	
15 Romania		**44** Central African Rep.	
16 Hungary		**45** Gabon	
17 Slovakia		**46** Congo	
18 Czech Rep.		**47** Lesotho	
19 Russian Fed.		**48** Swaziland	
20 Belarus		**49** Zimbabwe	
21 Lithuania		**50** Malawi	
22 Latvia		**51** Burundi	
23 Estonia		**52** Rwanda	
24 Moldova		**53** Uganda	
25 Georgia		**54** Djibouti	
26 Armenia		**55** Eritrea	
27 Azerbaijan		**56** U.A.E.	
28 Uzbekistan		**57** Qatar	
29 Kyrgyzstan		**58** Kuwait	

ctic Ocean

Finland

den

Russia

23
22
19 **21**
20

oland

17 Ukraine
16
9 **15** **24**
10 **12** **14**
11 **13**
Greece **25** Turkmenistan **28** **29**
26 **27**
Turkey **30**
33 **32** **31**
34 Iraq Iran Afghanistan
35 **58**

bya
Egypt
Saudi **57** **56**
Arabia
Oman

Chad **55**
Sudan Yemen
54
Ethiopia

44

16
Dem Rep. **52**
of Congo **51**
Tanzania

ngola
Zambia **50**
49
Botswana
ibia **48**
47
Rep. of
outh Africa

Kazakhstan

Mongolia

N. Korea

S. Korea Japan

China

Nepal
Bhutan
Bangladesh
Laos
Pakistan
India
Myanmar
Taiwan

Cambodia
Vietnam
Sri Lanka Thailand Brunei

Somalia

53 Kenya

Madagascar

Philippines

Pacific Ocean

Malaysia
I n d o n e s i a
Papua
New
Guinea

Indian Ocean

Australia

New Zealand

Southern Ocean

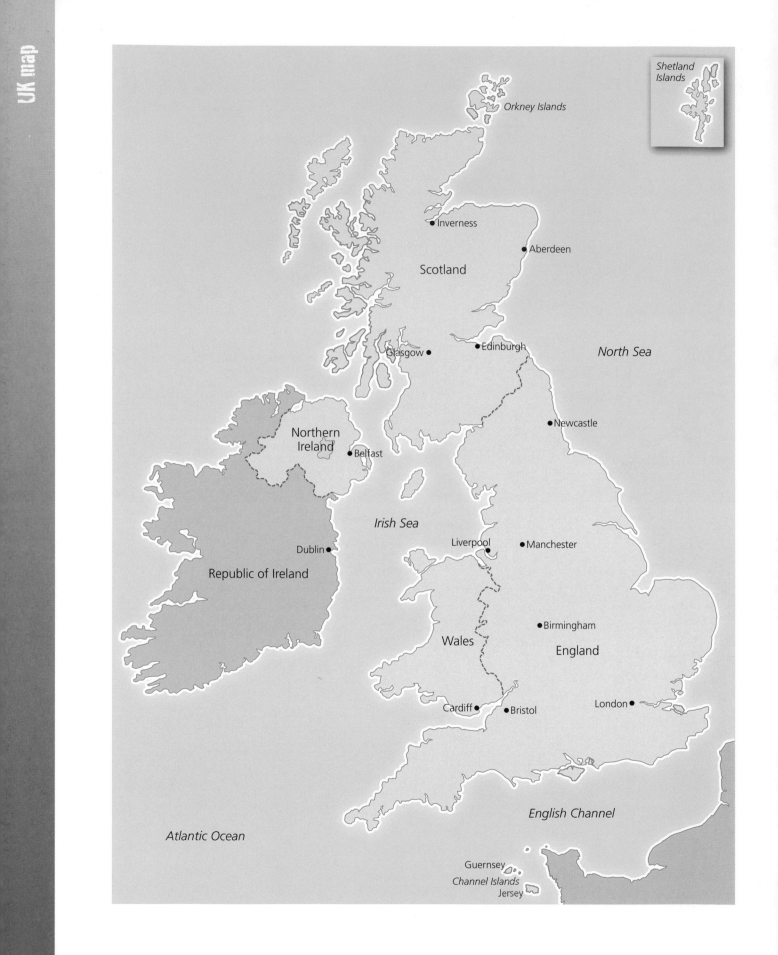

Shetland Islands

Orkney Islands

• Inverness

• Aberdeen

Scotland

North Sea

Glasgow • • Edinburgh

Northern
Ireland

• Newcastle

• Belfast

Irish Sea

Liverpool • • Manchester

Dublin •

Republic of Ireland

• Birmingham

Wales

England

Cardiff • • Bristol

London •

English Channel

Atlantic Ocean

Guernsey
Channel Islands
Jersey

Curriculum for Excellence mapping grid

Curriculum for Excellence Social Studies Level 4 Experiences and Outcomes

Chapter	People, past events and societies												People, place and environment													People in society, economy and business																			
	SOC 4-01a	SOC 4-02a	SOC 4-04a	SOC 4-04b	SOC 4-04c	SOC 4-05a	SOC 4-05b	SOC 4-05c	SOC 4-06a	SOC 4-06b	SOC 4-06c	SOC 4-06d	SOC 4-07a	SOC 4-08a	SOC 4-09a	SOC 4-09b	SOC 4-10a	SOC 4-10b	SOC 4-10c	SOC 4-11a	SOC 4-11b	SOC 4-11c	SOC 4-12a	SOC 4-12b	SOC 4-12c	SOC 4-14a	SOC 4-15a	SOC 4-16a	SOC 4-16b	SOC 4-16c	SOC 4-17a	SOC 4-17b	SOC 4-17c	SOC 4-18a	SOC 4-18b	SOC 4-18c	SOC 4-19a	SOC 4-19b	SOC 4-20a	SOC 4-20b	SOC 4-20c	SOC 4-21a	SOC 4-21b	SOC 4-22a	SOC 4-22b
1																																					■								
2																																■													
3																															■	■													
4																																■													
5																																													
6																													■					■											
7																																								■					
8																											■		■																
9																																								■					
10																											■		■																
11																											■		■																
12					■																																								
13																											■	■								■	■								
14																												■																	
15																																			■										
16																															■			■	■										
17																																		■											
18																											■					■		■											
19																																		■											
20																																		■					■						■
21																																										■	■		
22																																													■
23																																												■	■
24																				■																			■						■
25																												■						■											

124

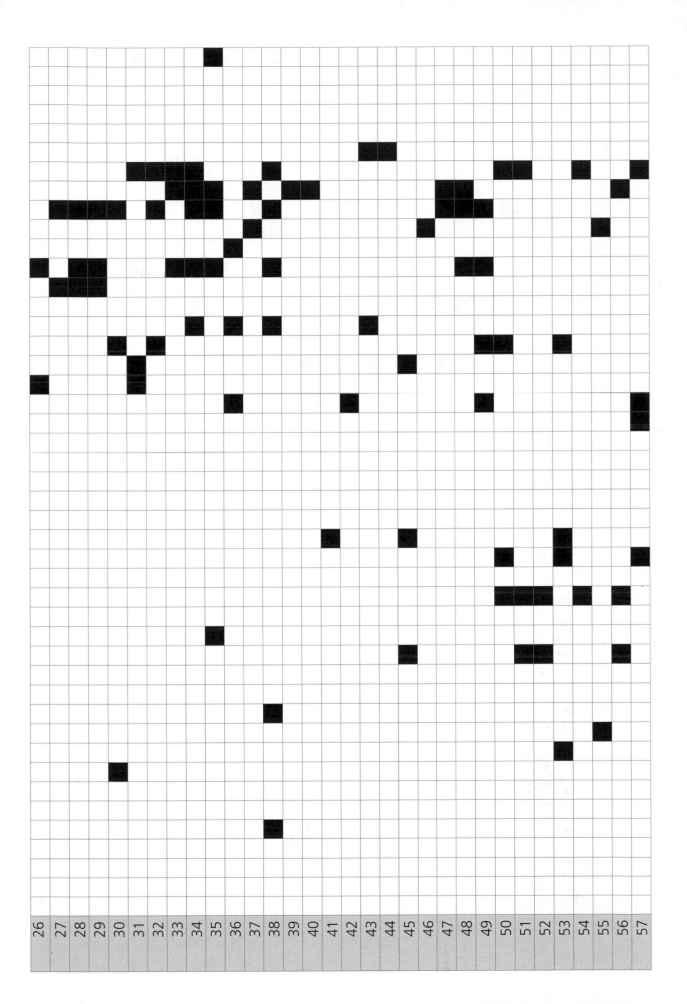